The Wanted Man

Between 1983 and 1986, the Bob Dylan Information Office that I had co-founded in 1981 with John Bauldie, Dave Dingle and other friends – known to one and all as Wanted Man – published five monographs in its own, self-proclaimed Study Series.

Each volume, according to the series editor, the late John Bauldie, was supposed to be a 'stud[y] of [an] individual LP record by Bob Dylan, or of particular themes in Bob Dylan's written and recorded work'.

The first two volumes published were indeed devoted to specific albums: John Hinchey's fine essay on *Slow Train Coming* and John B.'s own monograph on Dylan's 'other' mid-seventies masterpiece, *Desire*. The intention was to produce work with an academic rigour outside of the rigid confines of academia, which back then was wholly disinterested in Dylan.

If academia has slowly woken up to Dylan's cultural and artistic importance in the intervening decades – so much so that there is now an Institute of Dylan Studies at the University of Tulsa – the rigour that these Wanted Men displayed then (and now) is still disappointingly hard to find inside most mausoleums of higher learning.

As such, methinks now is the time to revive the Wanted Man Study Series, beginning with an account of what many fans consider the greatest of 'individual LP records by Bob Dylan': *Blood On The Tracks*; in it, I draw on new first-hand interviews and access to the full session histories for the original, so-called 'New York' album, recorded between September 16th and the 19th, 1974.

It is hoped that the rebirth of the Study Series will prompt others to follow in the footsteps of John Hinchey, Aidan Day, Nick de Somogyi and Bert Cartwright, submitting further potential volumes to myself – as John's successor in the role of self-appointed series editor – via Route Books, our new publisher. After all, as the mercurial bard himself said, 'You can kill a man, but you can't kill an idea.'

– Clinton Heylin, September 2018.

No One Else Could Play That Tune

The Making and Unmaking of Bob Dylan's 1974 Masterpiece

Clinton Heylin

Wanted Man Study Series
Take II ~ Vol. 1

route

First published by Route in 2018
PO Box 167, Pontefract, WF8 4WW
info@route-online.com
www.route-online.com

ISBN : 978-1-901927-76-4

FIRST EDITION, 1000 copies

Cover design:
Baker

Printed & bound in Great Britain by T.J. International Ltd

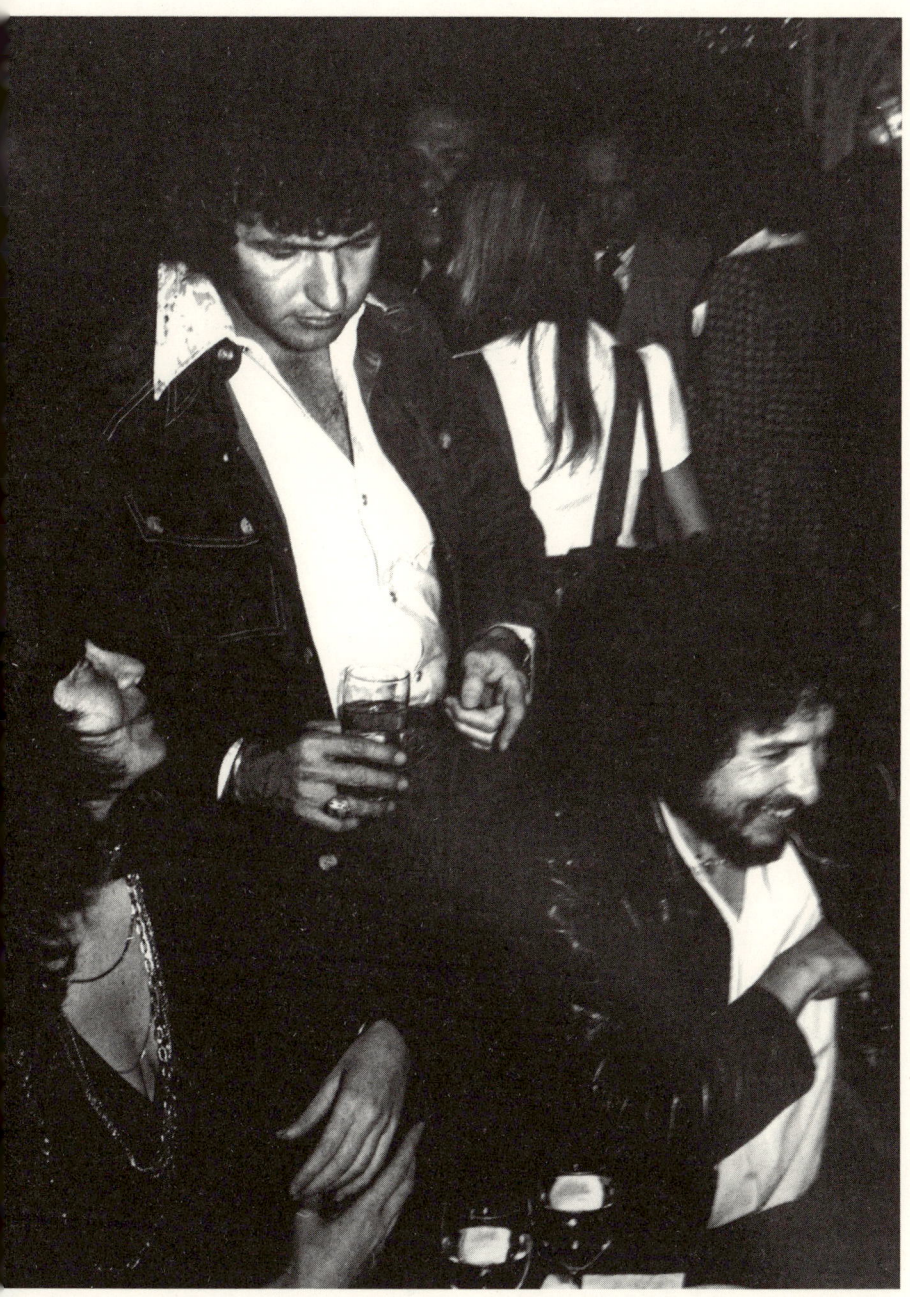

(i)

And I could never let you go,
No matter what goes on,
'Cause I love you more than ever,
Now that the past is gone.
        —The last verse of the final song on the album which
precedes *Blood On The Tracks*, 'Wedding Song', November 1973.

I helped her out of a jam, I guess
But I used a little too much force.
        —'Tangled Up In Blue', 1974.

I wrote all the songs for Blood On The Tracks *in about a month and then I recorded*
them and stepped back out of that place where I was when I wrote them and went
back to whatever I was doing before. Sometimes you'll get what you can out of these
things, but you can't stay there.
        —Bob Dylan to Bill Flanagan, *Written In My Soul*, March 1985.

In the end, it's an album that has touched us all; not confining itself
to the Oran of Camus, wherever the hell that may be; even appealing
to supporters of the 'men in sharkskin suits, who [run] for President
promising life and delivering death'. And it does so by 'retreat[ing]
into that past that never was'; a place where Fred Astaire won the girl,
only to lose her in the next movie before winning her back again,
ad infinitum. The divine comedy of errors.

If *Blood On The Tracks* really is the product of a 'land where the
poets died', that land was Abyssinia, not America, where Rimbaud
'started into dealing with slaves and something inside of him died',
a place Conrad equated with the heart of darkness. It stands as an
endlessly beguiling mosaic, not merely multi-layered but infinitely
renewable. And yet, one can't help but wonder what might have
been...

★★★

Theoretically, much of the heavy lifting has already been done when it comes to the story of *Blood On The Tracks*, most of it in the 21st century. An entire book on the making of this iconic album, co-authored by one of its more erudite participants, Minneapolis musician Kevin Odegard, was published in 2004 by Da Capo Press.

Despite co-author Andy Gill's turgid prose style and penchant for speculative generalising whenever information dried up, *A Simple Twist Of Fate* displayed plentiful evidence of Odegard's diligence. Interviewing almost all of the musicians and the two overseers, Phil Ramone and Paul Martinson, of the New York and Minneapolis sessions respectively, Odegard unlocked a familiar narrative of communal frustration at Dylan's idiosyncratic ways.

This theme also endures in the two other published eyewitness accounts of the New York sessions which followed in Odegard's wake. Legendary producer Phil Ramone devoted a slim chapter to the sessions in his insubstantial 2007 autobiography, *Making Records*, adding almost nothing to the account he previously gave Odegard.

Indeed, he devoted fully half of said chapter to an anecdote from pedal steel player Buddy Cage about how Dylan played mind games to get him to up his game when overdubbing 'Meet Me In The Morning'.

Unfortunately, said story inhabits the same parallel universe as one from Eric Weissberg's band Deliverance, drummer Richard Crooks, when he suggested, 'We were only there for three days and then we were gone.' If Crooks did hang around – and an offhand comment suggests he *might* have been at the mixing session on September 18th – he was only actually called on to play for some three hours, recording four songs.

Also there was Barry Kornfeld, an old friend of Dylan's who had last recorded with the man in 1963. Even if Weissberg's band collectively deny his presence, the AFM sheets prove Kornfeld *was* there but, although he got paid, he never got to play.

When I questioned bassist Tony Brown – the only man to play on all three sessions from which the original album was culled – regarding Dylan's decision to switch between recording semi-acoustic and taping with the full band, he denied such a thing ever happened.

Only after I informed him that I had seen all the studio logs – and there was no doubt about the recording sequence – did he express surprise at the trick his memory was playing with him: 'You think I would have [remembered], because it would have been so uncomfortable … Because he's *dissing* those guys.' Which he was.

Perhaps there was someone whom Odegard had somehow overlooked, who remembered things better. It took ten years to find a possible candidate, before 2014 saw a blog by the assistant engineer on these fabled New York sessions, Glenn Berger, republished in *Esquire* (of all places). Though his memory also sometimes played tricks, Berger did come up with perhaps the most apposite description to date of what happened across those four days in September:

> Dylan cut the whole thing in six hours on a Monday night … Then Dylan came back in on Tuesday, and recorded most of the album again. This time he had Paul Griffin, the keyboard player … That seemed to work, but it turned out not … On [the] Thursday, we recorded the album for a third time, this time just with the bass.

It's an immediately arresting idea, and one the tapes in essence bear out. However, Berger revealed during e-mail exchanges that he wasn't actually the assistant engineer on the final session that Thursday (or, it turned out, on the Wednesday). His friend and fellow assistant to Ramone, Rich Blakin, was occupying his chair, even if Berger evidently popped in.

At least Berger was willing – with the benefit of hindsight – to celebrate the sheer historic nature of those four days at A & R Studios, unlike his embittered erstwhile boss, Ramone. But just as with the musicians who played on the 'New York album' and its nominal producer, when Berger ventures into specifics, four-decade old memories can betray him. Don't they all of us?

(I stand equally accused. In *Still On The Road: The Songs Of Bob Dylan 1974-2009*, I suggest that the only rational explanation for Dylan supposedly recording 'Call Letter Blues', then 'Meet Me In The Morning', then 'Call Letter Blues' at the first New York session was that the second take was in fact 'Call Letter Blues' – as the original studio-sheet suggested – over which Dylan later dubbed a new vocal. Er, not so. I should have considered Dylan's tendency to throw his fellow musicians curve balls, a process Berger confirms, 'He changed songs midstream. Notice how I cross[ed] out take three on "[If You See Her, Say] Hello" and write in the new title "Big Girl".')

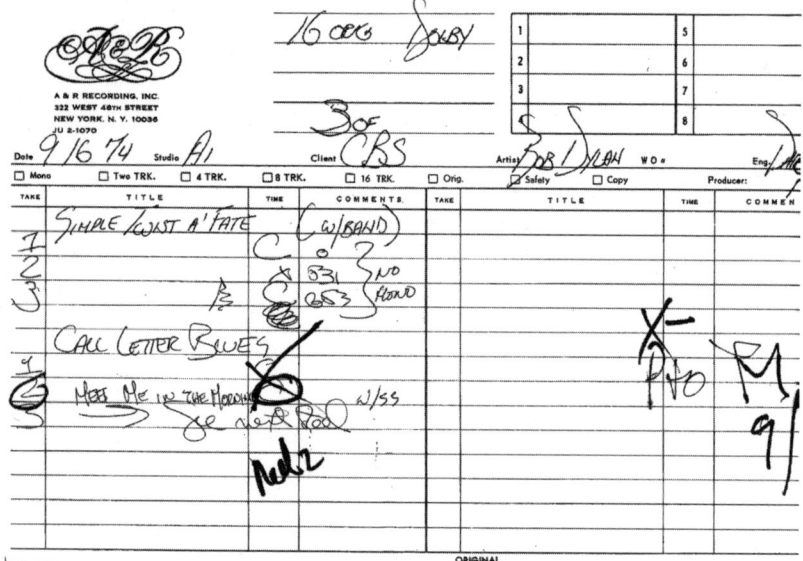

★★★

Inevitably, for all of us prior commentators, the session tapes – about to be released in their entirety – now serve as witnesses for the prosecution. Once thought to have been lost, the New York session multitracks have thankfully all survived – unlike their Midwest Yuletide kith and kin! They provide a welcome twist of fate given the paucity of contemporary documentation. (Not that one would expect to find a great deal of contemporary reportage, given the levels of secrecy and paranoia surrounding every post-accident Dylan studio session.)

In the intervening years, the one person who might have been expected to be called on to explain his thinking should have been the artist himself. But Dylan has been obliged to say surprisingly little about the making (and unmaking) of his greatest album, though he tantalisingly suggested he wrote a draft chapter on the subject for 2004's selective memoir, *Chronicles*.

In part, this is because during the period 1974-76 – which coincided with his commercial peak: three consecutive number one albums Stateside – Dylan granted almost no media interviews, and the few that he did (Travers, Jerome, Sloman, Hickey) steered a wide berth around the subject while the wounds were still raw. Only Mary Travers, an old friend from Peter, Paul & Mary days, raised the subject at a time when the resultant album was still riding high in the Hot Hundred. She was quickly shut down:

Mary Travers: One of the things I enjoyed about *Blood On The Tracks* as an album was that it was very simple.
Bob Dylan: Well, that's the way things are really. They are basically very simple. A lot of people tell me they enjoy that album. It's hard for me to relate to that. I mean, you know, people enjoying [that] type of pain.

Travers knew this was Bobspeak for, 'Can we move on?' And they did. Later in the year, Larry Sloman – whose November 1974 feature in *Rolling Stone* provided the only contemporary account of the New York sessions in print, leading to an invite on the 1975 Rolling Thunder Revue – had the chance to ask Dylan some questions for his own fine Rolling Thunder tome (*On The Road With Bob Dylan*), but ventured no further, at least not on the record.

Only in 1978 would his most critically acclaimed seventies album be addressed by reporters again and again; Dylan providing assorted bulletins on the influence of art teacher Norman Raeben and occasional references to the motifs from 'Tangled Up In Blue' in *Renaldo & Clara*. In one instance he even mentioned the supposed influence of Joni Mitchell's *Blue* on 'Tangled Up In Blue', while discussing his favourite mid-seventies songs with Craig McGregor in Brisbane, only for McGregor to omit the most intriguing part of the conversation from his published text:

Craig McGregor: Which songs from the last few years are you close to?
Bob Dylan: A bunch of 'em off *Blood On The Tracks*. Half a dozen off *Desire*. 'Knockin' on Heaven's Door' is a good song…
CM: Which are the ones on *Blood On The Tracks*?
BD: 'Idiot Wind'. 'Big Girl Now'. 'Tangled Up In Blue'.
CM: I always thought 'Tangled Up In Blue' was a great song.
BD: Me, too.

In interviews at opposite ends of that year of intense activity, Dylan addressed the past as the album's overarching theme and considered whether it qualified as a confessional work:

Bob Dylan: I don't think seriously about the past, the present or the future. I've spent enough time thinking about these things and have gotten nowhere.
Jonathan Cott: But didn't you when you wrote *Blood On The Tracks*? Why is it so intense?
Bob Dylan: Because there's physical blood in the soul, and flesh and blood are portraying it to you. Will power. Will power is what makes it an intense album … certainly not anything to do with the past or the future. [January 1978]

Matt Damsker: It seemed like *Blood On The Tracks* was a confession, it was real personal, it was a real chronicle…
Bob Dylan: Well, here's the thing. There might be some little

part of me which is confessing something which I've experienced and I know. But it is definitely not the total me confessing [to] *anything*. [September 1978]

After this, and an imminent religious conversion, the press seemed too obsessed with his current eschatological position to raise the matter until it had been firmly pushed into the past by an artist pressing on, even reconfiguring 'Tangled Up In Blue' to reflect that ongoing narrative ('Me, I'm still heading towards the Son').

As a result, our understanding of the journey from notebook/s to artifact has remained firmly in the foothills, just past base camp. Thankfully, help is finally at hand. As the prospect of an all-encompassing *Bootleg Series* devoted to the original sessions in New York looms, the mountain-top no longer looks so distant or so daunting.

★★★

Blood On The Tracks was conceptualised in advance – unlike any of its Columbia predecessors save perhaps that eponymous debut, which he did conceptualise, only for producer John Hammond to assert himself in the sequencing and song selection. The sifting process which usually took place in the studio, this time occurred before Dylan entered A & R.[1]

Even the recording process – while ostensibly resembling the one he'd utilised on *Bringing It All Back Home* – was framed by a more cogent conceit. The 1974 album was essentially always going to be ten songs – with just two slots open to negotiation: 'Call Letter Blues' versus 'Meet Me In The Morning', a debate that ended the minute Buddy Cage overdubbed pedal steel on the pair of 'em; and 'Up To Me' versus 'Buckets Of Rain', a debate which endured up until the mixing stage.

Otherwise, track *selection* was smooth as a rhapsody, with Ellen Bernstein occasionally waving the baton. Bernstein was the Columbia A&R lady who had become Dylan's latest romantic fixation and his constant companion while the (original, New York) album was being made:

Ellen Bernstein: As he wrote the songs and as he played them for the people [he knew], the sequencing decided itself … He was really definite when he went in [the studio]. He knew what he was going to do and he knew how he was going to do it.

All of which reflects a most unDylanlike *modus operandi*. He knew he had to cut this one fast, while the emotions were raw and the wounds open. He was making an *artistic* decision to air some dirty laundry in public for the first time in ten years, knowing that the era of the confessional album was upon him and speculation would soon be rife.

---

[1] The only other 20th century Dylan album to which this applies is that other 'marriage break-up' album, *Street-Legal,* with 'New Pony' the one last minute addition, à la 'Meet Me In The Morning'. This pre-selection may even have been what Dylan was referring to – sorting the wheat from the chaff – when he came up with the 1974 album's original title, *Threshing Floor.*

In the end, legitimate concerns would contribute to his ill-advised decision to rerecord half the album in his home state. With such songs he needed to not just feel the pain, but also communicate it, and not worry himself about making an album for 'people enjoying that type of pain'.

Yet he was determined not to make the same mistake he had made with *Another Side Of Bob Dylan* – writing the bulk of that album in a blaze of hurt and acrimony at the end of his torrid relationship with Suze Rotolo, during a ten-day break in Greece, and then taking what were little more than first drafts into the studio; recording the results in a single wine-suffused night. Not surprisingly, some of the resulting album, as one critic witheringly noted, felt a lot like reading somebody else's mail.

This time Dylan would go to considerable lengths to ensure he did more than record first drafts. Having a notebook full of songs to play – and ultimately record – was merely the starting point. What he needed now was the kind of feedback he had eschewed – for the first time – on *Another Side*.

Before that highly personal album he had always invoked the madding crowd of would-be singer-songwriters-cum-folksingers who toted their own guitars around the Village. In those halcyon days, when he wrote a new song there was always someone around to critique it (and, often as not, record it). It was in such an inferno of collective creativity Dylan became the songwriter he was destined to be.

By the time he had all but relocated to Woodstock in the summer of 1964, his was a name on the tip of even Fab Four tongues. But with that first bucolic retreat, he removed himself from the furnace of feedback in which he had previously burnished his work.

Perhaps the last non-Band member Dylan prepped with his latest songs before recording them was guitarist Michael Bloomfield, who travelled up to Woodstock in June 1965 to learn the basic structures of the works which would make up Dylan's commercial breakthrough, *Highway 61 Revisited* (before which he was informed the *auteur* didn't want 'any of that B.B. King shit').

Imagine Bloomfield's surprise when, nine summers later, Dylan turned up at his San Francisco apartment, wanting to play him the songs he'd written for his next album. Bloomfield described the scene that greeted him to Larry 'Ratso' Sloman, the following year:

Michael Bloomfield: Someone from Columbia phoned and ... they told me that no one could come by the house ... It was very uncomfortable with Bob and very intimidating. You know how Bob sorta taps his foot, man, like ... very hyper ... it makes you feel very uncomfortable, like [he's saying], let's get on with it. But get on with what? I couldn't correspond. I tried with all my soul and [then] I read ... how Eric Weissberg and the guys that played on *Blood On The Tracks* couldn't correspond either ... The same thing happened to them, they couldn't play either ... [Instead] he took out his guitar, he tuned to open D tuning and he started playing the songs non-stop ... He just played them all and I just sorta picked along ... Any attempt I made to say, 'Hey Bob, stop! Do it from the beginning so I [can] learn it,' or, 'Let me write a chart up, play it for me just verse and chorus,' [fell on stony ground.] But see, he was selling the whole song, and they weren't short songs. He was singing the whole thing and I was saying, 'No man, don't sing the whole thing, just sing one chorus and if it's not gonna change let me write it down, so I can play it with you.' [But] he didn't. He just kept on playing ... one after another and I got lost. They all began to sound the same to me. They were all in the same key, they were all long. I don't know, it was one of the strangest experiences of my life. And it really hurt ... He was sorta pissed that I didn't pick it up ... Maybe I just wasn't a quick enough study ... but if I was gonna teach somebody my tunes, I wouldn't do it that way. I would sit there [playing] slowly until they got it and then I would play it with them and when it was right, we'd know it ... But it made me feel weird ... I just felt this big wall, this enormous barrier that was so tangible that there was no way you could say, 'Hey man, how are you? You getting much pussy? Drinking a lot still? How are your kids?'

Nor was Dylan's appearance at Bloomfield's door a one-off whim. The handful of people he selected to hear these songs in their primordial state were contemporaries or near-contemporaries, usually people whose songwriting and/or instrumental dexterity he admired.

The one time Ellen accompanied him to such a session was when he visited Shel Silverstein on his houseboat. Dylan had long been an admirer of Silverstein's songwriting, which had yielded folk like Johnny Cash ('A Boy Named Sue') and Dr Hook ('Sylvia's Mother' &c.) country-rock hits.

Silverstein was extremely gracious and delighted by all the songs he heard. Such was not the case, though, when the first of the Laurel Canyon egotists was privileged enough to hear the new benchmark. Stephen Stills was staying at the St. Paul Hilton after a Crosby, Stills, Nash and Young show on July 22nd, when Dylan left his Minnesota farm long enough to say hello. A later bandleader of Bob's would prove the more attentive listener that evening:

Tim Drummond: He played us all the songs from *Blood On The Tracks* on acoustic guitar. We were on twin beds, across from each other. Oh God, I can't tell you how great it was. At one point Stephen said something to him about the songs not being good. I was so goddamn embarrassed. He was probably coked out. Dylan, being the ... man that he was, said, 'Well, Stephen, play me one of your songs.' That was the end of it. Stephen couldn't even find one string from another at that point.

According to Monica Bay, arts and entertainment editor of the *University of Minnesota Daily*, Dylan ended up playing twelve new songs for Stills and Drummond. He certainly had most of the songs by now, though he was still undecided about which would work in the studio and, crucially, on record.[2]

After this, Dylan took at least one more trip to San Francisco, even as he was already sequencing the songs in his head while continuing to preview them for friends and other strangers. One such lucky soul was country picker Peter Rowan, who first met Dylan at Newport back in 1965, when he was a member of Bill Monroe and his Bluegrass Boys. Club 47 owner Betsy Siggins had done her best to persuade Rowan to 'hang out, [insisting] that Bob was a

[2] Based on the contents of the two working notebooks and the 'fair copy' notebook (see Appendix III), the songs written or completed on the farm comprised 'Belltower Blues', 'If You See Her, Say Hello', 'Call Letter Blues', 'Where Do You Turn?', 'It's Breakin' Me Up', 'Up To Me', 'Ain't It Funny' and 'Little Bit Of Rain'. It appears that seven of the songs on the album were probably already written.

friendly sort, but I was intimidated by the invisible wall that seemed to surround him'.

The next time their paths crossed, Dylan was in Nashville's famous Columbia Studio A, recording the last few songs for *Blonde On Blonde*. Rowan remembered it well enough, but it is unlikely Dylan did, which is why Rowan was as stunned as Bloomfield when he got a call from the man himself, eight and a half years down the line:

Peter Rowan: I had moved to Stinson Beach on the coast, north of San Francisco, where I was reunited with Earth Opera partner David Grisman. David was producing my two younger brothers, Christopher and Lorin, for Columbia Records. Dave and I were starting to jam with Jerry Garcia in what became the bluegrass band, Old & In The Way. I got a call from Seatrain lyricist, Jim Roberts, over in Bolinas. Bob Dylan had shown up at his door. [He] must have been on a walkabout from life as a rock and roller! Jim said that Bob was looking to replace his favourite guitar, which had been stolen. I had my treasured 1936 Martin 000 Sunburst guitar and [he wanted to know] did I maybe want to sell it to Bob? Well, Bob got on the line and we talked. But I still thought it was a hoax, a prank, a joke on me. I gave Bob directions how to find my place, Old Sheriff Selmer's barn-workshop-home. 'Yeah, ya just follow the Bolinas Lagoon south and turn at the first unpaved road that heads towards the ocean, Stinson Beach. Call from the phone booth right there.' So he called. 'Okay, ya see that wooden tower just to your right? Drive up and park in front of it, the big yellow barn. Calle del Ribera. That's me upstairs in the window!' I watched the blue van pull up. Out stepped a man in brown corduroy clothes and cap. I watched him find his way and listened to his footsteps on the wooden stairs. In the room was my partner Leslie, and Milan and Mimi Melvin (aka Fariña), just returned from Tibet. We were used to visits from various world travellers and alias members of the Free Mexican Airforce. We waited. Only Bob's nose entered the doorway, sensing like radar the vibes! I went to greet him, he seemed taller than expected, wearing shades. 'Someplace we can go?' he asked quietly. We went downstairs to the empty front room with ocean light filling it. We both were wearing Ray-Ban shades against the glare of the wave-tossed sea outside. I took the old Martin 000 out of the case and handed it to him. He strummed it gently and hummed a melody. He handed it back and said, 'Here, you play it.' Really? So I sang him one of my songs, and asked him for one. He took the guitar and started to sing all the material from the unreleased *Blood On The Tracks*. We sat there for hours trading songs. The ocean outside with wild-horse waves, the glinting afternoon light reflecting on the old wooden walls of the room. It grew dark, and still the songs came! My brother [Lorin] showed up. It was dark and the candle lit, and still he wore his shades, so I kept mine on! Upstairs was silent, not a shoe scrape. 'Hey, ya know where Jerry Garcia lives?' And he went on his way in the blue van ... Late the next day I went up to Garcia's house and his wife Caroline – [the] 'Mountain Girl' – and I were talking. I tapped an ash into a full ashtray and she said, 'Careful, those butts are Dylan's cigarettes!'

Rowan had crossed Dylan's radar again because of his association with Grisman, with whom Dylan had recently started taking mandolin lessons. The loss of his favourite Martin, meanwhile, would resonate throughout the rest of 1974.

As Ellen recalls, 'The guitar was stolen from his van when it was parked in front of my house in Mill Valley ... We went around town putting up notes asking people to call if they knew anything about the whereabouts of the guitar that I believe David Bromberg had given him ... He was truly upset to lose the guitar.'

The loss of the guitar on which he had written this extraordinary body of songs was something Dylan would come to interpret as one more cruel twist of fate, even as he euphemistically informed John Mankiewicz in 1978 that he'd 'left it behind. I'd squeezed it dry.' In truth, he was still trying to replace it when he turned up at Sound 80 studios in Minneapolis two days after Christmas, hoping to reproduce the vibe the songs had when he still had his trusted Martin.

★★★

The theme of returning [would] run through the sessions.
                                    —Ellen Bernstein to author.

He remained with Ellen through August and into September, enjoying their time together, shaping his best set of songs in years and seeking shelter from another storm which he knew was due to break in early August, when CBS used its annual convention in LA to announce they had re-signed Dylan (and Barbra Streisand) to the label. The chastening sight of *Planet Waves* at the top of the *Billboard* charts, Dylan's first ever US number one album, had forced a rethink.

Clandestine negotiations between Dylan's lawyer, David Braun, and CBS lawyer Elliot Goldman had been going on for months, preceding Dylan's delivery of the eagerly-awaited tour album to Asylum.

So when the announcement came – with *Before The Flood*, Dylan's second Asylum album, still riding high in the *Billboard* charts – it introduced David Geffen to a rare emotion: gall. For the first time he had been outmaneuvered by an artist he believed he had successfully wooed. Not so. Dylan had learnt the tricks of the trade from a true master, Albert Grossman, and knew a close relative of Diamond Jim the minute he entered a room.

Indeed, the *Billboard* report on Dylan's re-signing went so far as to suggest Dylan had 'apparently expressed displeasure about the spate of media stories hailing … Geffen as a genius'. According to the leading music-industry weekly, 'Dylan was extremely displeased with total sales tallies of … *Planet Waves,* due to heavy returns after an unprecedented publicity wave for his spring tour comeback with The Band petered out … [Also,] Dylan reportedly told staffers that he felt far more comfortable dealing with personnel whom he'd known for over a decade.'

The piece concluded with a hint that Dylan was in a hurry to release his fourth album in a year: '[He] is reported to have a number of songs ready for his next album, although studio dates and producer assignment are not yet set.'

In reality, CBS's headline-grabbing announcement was a tad premature. Despite much trumpeting, the new contract was not a done deal, and Dylan had form when it came to walking away from an on-the-table contract with Columbia, something he had done when a three-album deal was offered in November 1971.

One of the major stumbling blocks at the final stage of negotiations that summer was Dylan's insistence he retain copyright and ownership of all unreleased masters, delivering to the label only finished albums from now on. In an internal memo dated August 9th, Elliot Goldman reported to his CBS boss, Don Biederman, that the artist was proving implacable on this particular point:

> In the final analysis, Braun and Naomi Saltzman very strongly resisted my position that any extra recordings made by Dylan while recording an album be owned by us, even though we could not use them. In the interests of closing the deal, recognizing the fact that with Dylan in creative control of the recordings he could keep these extra recordings and we would never know the difference, and lastly, in consideration of the fact that any delivery of product by Dylan to a third party terminates our deal and Dylan's supplemental royalties under the deal, I have yielded this point. In essence, Dylan will retain ownership of any outtakes recorded in conjunction with an album he is recording for delivery to us. However, Dylan cannot deal with those recordings during our period of exclusivity with him.

As far as Dylan was concerned, there would be no more albums like *Dylan* – a record compiled from the detritus discarded during the *Self Portrait* and *New Morning* projects – no matter how much he shrugged off the audible sound of an album scraping the bottom of the barrel in conversation.[3]

Facing up to the inevitable, Columbia had little choice but to capitulate. Dylan was no longer the greenhorn who signed his 1961 contract without legal representation and still under the legal age of consent. More important, he was returning home, bringing with him a set of songs capturing a time when 'revolution [was] in the air'.

Dylan had even returned to frequenting New York, three thousand miles due east of the LA asylum. As he told Jim Jerome, the following October, 'I live where I have to live, where my priorities are … Right now it is [in New York], and [has been] off and on since last spring.'

[3] Dylan's one on-the-record comment about the LP was to Ben Fong-Torres in January 1974: 'They were just not to be used. I thought it was well understood. They were just to warm up.'

And yet, this was not a 'New York' album. Most of the songs had been composed in the Bay Area when staying with Ellen, or on his Minnesota farm, when Ellen was staying with him. It was only in early September, when he was almost done, that they decamped to New York, staying at Shel Silverstein's apartment at 432 Hudson Street, rather than one of Dylan's townhouses – presumably seeking privacy while everything was put in place for his next studio sortie.

Such was Dylan's hurry to get started, he could barely wait for the ink to dry on the new CBS contracts. Dylan's long-standing lawyer, Braun, only returned the four signed contracts to CBS on Friday the 13th. The following Monday, his client began work on *Blood On The Tracks*.

★★★

In my kind of thing you have to have the proper instrument. I played acoustical songs on that Band tour in '74, but I pushed too hard. I played acoustical guitar on the Rolling Thunder tours, but I had to push too hard. And for my type of style I can't really afford to push too hard, because I lose the reason behind the song. If you heard me sittin' in a room singing, I wouldn't be pushing too hard.

—Bob Dylan to Craig McGregor, March 1978.

When Dylan entered the oh-so-familiar surroundings of Manhattan's A & R Studios at 799 7th Avenue on the Monday afternoon – September 16th, 1974 – he hoped to make a record that didn't sound like he was 'pushing too hard', but rather one akin to 'sitting in a room singing' to friends.

It had been a long time since he had felt this sure of a set of songs or this focused on how he might go about such a Sisyphean task. Sure, he had been here before, but not in a while.

Planet Waves had been recorded in a hurry. Not just quickly, but in a hurry. And the pattern of writing songs *in situ* to complete an album had been one he had adhered to throughout the post-accident era. But this time he had a whole album, not just a half.

It had been his most productive summer since that *annus mirabilis* 1967, when he had written and recorded two albums' worth of originals in The Band's large pink garage, only to record an entirely different album in six weeks that fall, the inspiringly austere, positively august *John Wesley Harding.*

That had been the last time he had entered a studio knowing what he was going to record and promptly recorded it in three days. That album, though, had not been the product of a single set of sessions. Dylan had required three separate trips to Nashville to get all twelve songs and strip 'em bare.

Back in '67, he had been undecided whether to leave his first album of a new Columbia deal semi-acoustic. Initially, he was inclined to ask the band he'd kept on retainer for eighteen months to earn some daily crust by embellishing the simple guitar-bass-drums sound captured at those sessions. Robbie Robertson dissuaded him.

The 1974 album he was set to start recording on Rosh Hashanah was a very different beast. *Bringing It All Back Home* – the album he had recorded in three days in January 1965 at this very studio – was actually the closer cousin. After all, that was the last of his albums to include a whole side of acoustic songs.

It was also one he had begun acoustically, reverting to electric (and semi-electric) for two and a half sessions, only to revert to acoustic, cutting the entire second half of the album in a single afternoon, having already previewed the three key songs in concert (a practice Dylan subsequently abandoned, apparently afraid commercial bootleggers – who first put their head above the parapet in the summer of '69 – would steal his thunder).

How ironic, therefore, that the half an album he recorded in September 1974 but subsequently scrapped should appear on bootleg only a matter of weeks after he (again) second-guessed himself; releasing a reconfigured record quite different from the record he initially approved.

Of course, re-recording and reconfiguring albums had always been part of the man's DNA, and would continue to be, well into the noughties. Famously, Columbia had accidentally released his sophomore album *Freewheelin'* in its original guise in May 1963, before it was hastily recalled.

New Morning was another artifact Dylan sequenced and mixed, only to return to the studio to record one new track ('Day Of The Locusts'), and promptly re-recording two more. Even *Dylan* – the CBS 'revenge' album released as a 'spoiler' a fortnight before the man's 1974 comeback tour – had a different sequence when announced to the press in October 1973.[4]

Not that any of these would ever attract the interest – or generate quite the debate – the so-called 'New York' *Blood On The Tracks* has; perhaps because nothing he had done to those LPs fundamentally changed the nature of these respective collections. Such would be the case this time – hence 'the making *and unmaking* of Dylan's masterpiece'.

---

[4] 'Running' and 'Alligator Man', the two substituted tracks, both remain unreleased despite a two-CD Bootleg Series, *Another Self Portrait*, from these sessions in 2013.

(ii)

Modern recording technology never endeared itself to me. My kind of sound is very simple ... A little bit of echo ... that's about all that's required to record it.
—Bob Dylan to Greg Kot, August 1993.

You know the studios in the old days were all much better, and the equipment so much better, there's no question about it in my mind. You just walked into a studio, they were just big rooms, you just sang, you know, you just made records; and they sounded like the way they sounded there. That stopped happening in the late sixties, for me anyway.
—Bob Dylan to Bono, July 8th, 1984.

One thing is certain – when Dylan entered the old Studio A shortly before 4pm on this particular Monday afternoon, he was looking to make as musically understated an album as possible. For that, he would need to go back to the way he used to make records back in the day, in surroundings both familiar and musically warm. As Ellen cogently observes, 'The sound of the album was such a return that it made a lot of sense to do it there.'

If there was wild mercury in any studio in New York, it was at A & R, where both producer/engineer Phil Ramone and assistant engineer Glenn Berger revelled in its pervasive sense of musical history:

Glenn Berger: A & R's Studio A-1 was on the seventh floor of 799 7th Avenue on 52nd Street in New York City. It had once been Columbia's studio, where Dylan had done his early work, [before] they had sold it to [Phil] Ramone and company in 1968 ... A-1 was a beautiful room that enchanted everyone who sang or played in it. It was a good size, 90-feet long, 60-feet wide, with 30-foot ceilings. From the street, you could see this big box with a peaked copper roof (the copper was there to keep out stray electronic interference), stuck on top of the building.

Phil Ramone: Dylan had an incredible love for this room, which had been sold by Columbia. A group of us, including me, ended up buying the studio, and we made a few changes, but not too many. It was a big room, just like a church, with a huge, high ceiling.

Here was the very place – rebranded, but intact – where Dylan had recorded every official artifact between November 20th, 1961 (*Bob Dylan*) and January 25th, 1966 ('One Of Us Must Know'). The sense of historical synergy was not lost on the one reporter diligent enough to reconstruct these sessions in real time. Larry Sloman's description in his November *Rolling Stone* piece set the scene perfectly:

> It looked like old times at Columbia's A & R Studio September 16th. John Hammond Snr. was there. Phil Ramone was working the board. Eric Weissberg and Barry Kornfeld, two old Gaslight regulars, were unpacking their guitars. And sitting out in the cavernous studio … practically hidden behind a battery of six microphones, Bob Dylan was creating another album. And it was almost as if Dylan were consciously conjuring up the ambience of the early sixties.

And Dylan's points of reference were not just his own. He had surely heard stories about the revamped A & R Studios from members of The Band, who had convened there in spring 1968 to record their own seminal debut, *Music From Big Pink*.

A year or more spent recording with Dylan in close proximity at their home studio, the Big Pink 'basement', had convinced the folk-rocker's former backing band their erstwhile boss's recording aesthetic made a lot of sense. It seems very likely that one or more of them would have regaled Dylan with a version of their experience at A & R similar to one related by Robbie Robertson in his 2016 memoir:

> John Simon had booked studio time for us in his favourite room at A & R Studios in the city. He suggested going in for just a few days at first to make sure it felt right … We loaded our equipment into A & R Studios with John [Simon]'s help. Don Hahn, the recording engineer, and his second, Shelly Yakus, showed us precisely where they wanted our instruments set up. They put our microphones and chairs where we would sit and arranged sound baffles between us. Don explained that this setup was what made this studio sound so

good. 'This is how we record everybody in this room. Tried and true, it works great.' They put blankets over the piano, set the bass amp behind a wall and mine facing away from me, and Garth's Leslie [organ] was padded and surrounded by glass. We followed all this protocol, wanting to be professional ... [But] halfway through the [first] song [it was obvious that] musically there was something terribly wrong. I put down my guitar on the floor and went into the control room. 'This doesn't work, John. Sorry, we can't record like this ... We can't make music with an isolated setup. We have to see one another. We have to read one another's signals. That's how we play – to each other.' ... John yelled into the control room at Don and Shelly, 'Okay guys, new setup. We're moving everything around ... We have to make these guys feel comfortable. I've seen them play music in their basement and that's what works for them, so we've got to try.' ... Now we could hear one another in the room and make eye contact ... We recorded 'Tears of Rage' ... and Don and Shelly said over the talk-back, 'You guys should come in and hear this. It's sounding real good.' ... With our unconventional recording setup in the studio and the lower-quality mics we were using, Don and Shelly asked their boss and chief engineer, Phil Ramone, to come in and check out our discovery. They showed him how we set up in a circle, with total eye contact. Some of our amps and speakers were a bit baffled but [we] were out in the open. Phil ... threw up his hands, like he couldn't believe this would work ... John smiled and pushed play on the tape machine. Phil sat down and listened intently to a couple of the songs we'd recorded, then looked at the engineers, looked at John, stood up and said, 'That's incredible. That's really fucking incredible.'

In fact, early A & R versions of 'In The Station', 'We Can Talk' and 'This Wheel's On Fire' found their way onto the very last basement reel – the one which included Dylan originals like 'Wild Wolf', 'Santa Fé' and 'Silent Weekend' – confirming just how intertwined the two projects had become during *Music From Big Pink*'s formative stages.

Although Phil Ramone would never produce The Band, he had resumed his association with the self-confident Canadians in February 1974, after the first hired hand to record the momentous Dylan/Band tour of that year, at New York's Madison Square Gardens, failed to mike up the snare drum.

When the project was revived at the West Coast tail end of the tour – the night Dylan met Ellen Bernstein backstage in Oakland – it was Ramone who was trusted with rolling tape; at tour's end, he then helped Ron Fraboni edit and sequence the tapes into a nominally satisfying souvenir tour sampler.

However, this was not the association which served as tipping-point for Ramone's pivotal role in the next chapter in Dylan's saga. Rather, as the producer later revealed to both Robbie Robertson and Kevin Odegard, it was the sound he had got on Paul Simon's second domestic solo album, *There Goes Rhymin' Simon*, released in May 1973, which set Dylan thinking he could achieve something similar using his own contradistinct methodology.

With *Rhymin' Simon*, Paul had prepared himself for the long haul, recording at five different studios and using three different (co-) producers: Ramone, Allen Touissant and someone who had been Dylan's engineer in the 'wild mercury' years and who was not shy of voicing his views on Dylan's antithetical aesthetic:

Roy Halee: Dylan was not easy to work with in the studio. He liked to do things very quick and very disorganized. He'd say, 'I want to do a vocal over here by the drums,' and stand next to the drummer. And you'd say, 'Hey, look, it's kinda hard to isolate you by the drums when … he's beating his brains out.' But he didn't care. [1990]

Dylan loved the warmth of sound on Simon's record. It was just what he was looking for.[5] He just didn't want to spend nine months getting it. He intended to complete his statement in a couple of days.

If something he said in 1978 can be believed, another album he had been playing a lot was Joni Mitchell's soul-baring *Blue*, which along with Carole King's *Tapestry* had almost defined the confessional-album-for-college-dorms genre at the start of the decade. Playing the album repeatedly, Dylan claimed 'it affected me, I couldn't get it out of my head. And it just stayed in my head.'

---

[5] In a *Rolling Stone* interview at the time of the sessions, Simon had implied he thought Dylan was washed up creatively: 'Dylan was great, I gotta say he was great. I don't feel that at the moment, but I feel that he was great,' a criticism that evidently smarted. Dylan retorted in 1975 that someone should 'tell Paul Simon … we're out here blazing new trails! What's Paul Simon ever written that means anything to anyone?'

It was a statement which later convinced an increasingly deranged Joni Mitchell that people were going around suggesting the original version of *Blood On The Tracks* was 'like a Joni Mitchell album'. They were not. Not even tin-eared angels could have heard the similarities, but it was a comparison the lady repeatedly made, perhaps still quietly seething at Dylan's response to her magical 1974 album, *Court and Spark* – feigning falling asleep when she played it for him.

If anything, it was this maturer work – Joni's most lyrically sophisticated album to date – which provided a more appropriate exemplar for such an overtly literate collection of songs as *Blood On The Tracks*, a case of Dylan reclaiming his compositional crown. He even planned to release his album on the first anniversary of *Court and Spark*'s release: New Year's Day 1975.

One leaf he certainly took from Simon, Mitchell et al. was asserting himself as *producer* of his own record/s – not just their *auteur*. He even went one step further. Whereas these two contemporaries were content to take co-production credits on their most recent albums, Dylan was determined to employ Ramone in the role of engineer alone. There would be no confusion as to who really was at the helm:

Ellen Bernstein: [Dylan] knew these songs. He knew his vision for these songs [which] was very pure and very unadorned, and you don't need a producer if your vision is that personal on something. I think he had a lot of belief in the integrity of the material.

Perhaps Dylan was already aware of the rep Ramone had started to acquire. According to *Blood On The Tracks* musician Charlie Brown III, Phil was someone who liked to take 'a lot of credit for stuff that I don't think he did. Producing all these people and having his name on it as producer is bullshit, because he didn't do anything, y'know.'

What Ramone certainly was, though, was a consummate engineer; as good at mastering the nuances of analogue sound as Halee, minus the attitude. And his brief was the same one Dylan shared with his original Columbia producer, John Hammond Snr., the very afternoon they both returned to A & R: 'I want to lay down a whole bunch of tracks. I don't want to overdub. I want it easy and natural.'

Ellen recalls how the veteran A&R man 'had asked to come into the studio that first night since it was historic in so many ways for him *and* for Bob, [who] was very welcoming … It was a lovely moment.' Yet Hammond was slightly baffled by Dylan's choice of recording date, pointing out to his former protégé, 'This is a strange day to start recording … It is Rosh Hashanah and it is hard to get musicians.' Looking for his own new beginning, Dylan snapped back, 'Why not today? It's the new year, isn't it?'

Although A & R had a state-of-the-art sixteen-track desk, Dylan made it clear he intended to begin by recording a few songs acoustically, and that four tracks – the number he had used on every Studio A recording in the first half of the sixties – would suffice. Ramone suggested two guitar mikes and a single Sennheiser 421, a popular stage mike at the time, for the vocals:

Phil Ramone: I used the technique at the time … of using two guitar mikes, for reasons of sound and to give him freedom of movement, because he's not prone to stand in one place without moving around … We had pretty good isolation. You hear his voice in his guitar mike, as you would anyone's, but leakage is important, and the leakage in the guitar mike was quite good … I didn't use anything but a dynamic mike on his vocals. It helped with the isolation, too … How do you keep the vocal out of the guitar mike, or vice versa? … The Sennheiser 421 … had an interesting top end, a warmth, if you kept reasonably close to it.

Assistant engineer Glenn Berger recalled, in his studio memoir, scurrying around trying to get the set-up just right, before leading 'Dylan out to the studio and plac[ing] him in front of the mics. We used old Neumann microphones [sic], the kind he would've used in the early sixties.[6] I stood inches from him … [It was] the seventies. It wasn't the antiseptic spaceship of 2001. It was dirty and falling apart. It was all tubes, no transistors. The board would get hot … We had no idea what he was going to do, so we had to be ready for anything … As I ran around the studio tweaking mic positions, he called off a tune.

[6] Berger agrees that they did actually use the Sennheiser 421, further noting that 'the reason for using that mic is because it had a very tight pattern and picked up virtually no leakage from other mics, so if you were recording in a room with other cats it was a good mic to use.'

"Let's do 'Tangled Up In Blue' in G." He hit his guitar, but instead of a G chord, it was an A. He was playing in a different key from the one he had called off and the lyrics were [to] "If You See Her, Say Hello".'

The clock read just past four. If Dylan for even a moment thought about starting with 'Tangled Up In Blue' – in many ways the album's trigger – no evidence remains on the studio logs or tapes, even though they were running both a mono reference tape (at either 7½ or 15 ips), plus a regular 30 ips multitrack.[7]

When song one rolls, both reels record Ramone calling out, '"If You See Her, Say Hello" take one.' No mistake. A perfect starter – even though the song was one of the last Dylan wrote for the album. Entirely absent from the two working notebooks Dylan was using prior to his summer visit to the farm – both of which are now housed at the Dylan archive in Tulsa – the lyric appears only in the 'fair copy' notebook that remains at the Morgan Library, New York, the seventh (of fifteen) songs therein.[8]

It turns out 'If You See Her, Say Hello' had mutated from another song Dylan had been working on, only to scrap: 'There Ain't Gonna Be Any Next Time'. As his mood changed from autumnal brown to blue, he began to slip in lines like, 'So kiss her nice and say hello', 'Though the emptiness still lingers', and 'I respect her … for what she did'. If this soon-discarded paean was a *carpe diem* to his tardy self, its replacement would find him again ruing past mistakes and wracked with remorse.

On that very first take of 'If You See Her, Say Hello' – a marathon effort and stellar performance – he is already striving for the voice within and immediately captures the essence of *Blood On The Tracks*. Five and a half minutes long, it is punctuated by no fewer than four harmonica breaks.

With nary a pause, he goes in search of that voice again, this time reining himself in harmonica-lly, searching for a tonal breath control he can set to remote for the remainder of the sessions. He doesn't quite find it, but that second take is still 'pulled' to one of

[7] As we shall see, later that evening the mono reference tapes would capture some performances the multitrack missed, but for now they were running in tandem.

[8] After a close comparison of the two working notebooks, it seems clear that the order of the songs in said 'fair copy' notebook does not reflect the order in which they were written – save at the very end, when it stops being a 'fair copy' and reverts to being a working notebook for 'Idiot Wind', 'Up To Me' and a couple of fragments, one of which becomes 'Buckets Of Rain'.

three master reels at the end of the second session, from which Jeff Rosen evidently accessed this version when compiling 1991's *The Bootleg Series Vols. 1-3*.[9] Already, Dylan was in the forbidden zone – and Ramone sensed it:

Phil Ramone: This was a serious night … a very quiet, deliberate letting out of the inside of him. Emotionally, he was in a state of revealing his life. And most writers don't want to tell you they're writing their autobiography. But it's there in the atmosphere, as you hear the songs unfolding.

Ramone knew the stakes were high and the learning curve steep. It started with lesson one: 'Bob doesn't rehearse. Bob just starts creating [and] these songs start pouring out of him!'

In rapid succession, Dylan proceeds to reel off versions of 'You're A Big Girl Now' and 'Simple Twist Of Fate' that take him to the emotional core of a collection he has barely begun recording. This time both second takes have the edge on the first, even if a six-minute take one of 'You're A Big Girl Now' – with three seesaw bursts of the harmonica around his neck – prompts an impressed Ramone to correctly observe, 'Great song.'

It has always been assumed that 'Big Girl Now' was a song which set the stage for the album's inexorable arc: looking back at a love he stills feels for a woman after leaving a long-term relationship in tatters. Not so.

Among the mountain of Tulsa papers relating to this period is a single scrap of paper from the 1974 Tour with The Band, on which Dylan has rewritten 'Knockin' On Heaven's Door' and compiled a list of possible additions to the live set.

He has also written out, in telltale shorthand, the lyrics to a completed 'You're A Big Girl Now', which thus stands revealed as a companion-piece to 'Wedding Song', an expression of how much he is missing his wife on the road and his determination to be a better husband.[10] Things haven't quite come crashing down and he hasn't yet withdrawn.

---

[9] It appears only the takes pulled to master were accessed in 1991. It is certainly hard to believe that anyone but Dylan would have preferred this over the heartbreaking first take.
[10] Entries in the illustrated diary he kept on the road, now housed at the Morgan, confirm the pain this 'temporary' separation caused him in real time.

Nine months down the line, on a second A & R take of 'Big Girl', Dylan finally finds *the voice*; the one intended to define *Blood*'s better self, sung by someone who has risen above the hurt to make an album for the ages. Again, it is pulled to master (at the expense of a surprisingly stylized third take – cut after 'Simple Twist' – where he second-guesses himself).

Moving from one forensic examination of love and the pain of loss to another, Dylan comes to 'Simple Twist Of Fate'. Here is another chance to unlock an album which, in his own words, has taken him 'ten years to live and two years to write'.

'Tangled Up In Blue' – the song he introduced with the above phrase on the 1978 US tour – in its earliest draft, depicted a narrator who 'walks about the city block/ Like a skeleton that can hardly talk'.[11] By the time he relocated that couplet to 'Simple Twist Of Fate', the break-up presaged in 'Big Girl' was prompting him to think back to a Fourth Street affair twelve years earlier, and the last true love he lost; still unable to forget 'Suze and the way that she talked'.

Again, it takes just two takes to nail his heart to his sleeve. Pulled to master, this devastating second take prompts an approving response from the one sounding board Dylan is prepared to listen to. As the last note of another five-minute tour de force dies, Ellen hits the playback button and opines, 'That was great.'

To the others there for the duration, the lady was only ever ancillary to the process. As far as Ramone was concerned, on that first day, 'other than the musicians, the only people in the studio were Columbia's Don DeVito, John Hammond and me.' Assistant engineer Glenn Berger convinced himself it was Susan Blond, an Epic publicist, who was there at the outset.[12] As for Tony Brown, the bassist who played on the three main sessions, Ellen was simply 'a woman who … worked for Columbia'.

Berger's replacement as assistant engineer, Rich Blakin, was even more condescending, describing Ellen as 'a young lady who was sent over by CBS to be his girl Friday. Tea, phone calls, limo, etc.' The fact that she was to Blakin's left, 'seated at the producer's desk', seemed almost an affront to his own professional standing.

---

[11] This highly cinematic narrative always contained too many ideas for a single song. Hence, why some parts flew off and attached themselves to 'Idiot Wind' and 'Simple Twist Of Fate'.
[12] I asked the unbashful Blond, via a mutual friend, if she was there. She assured me she was not.

It never crossed Blakin's mind that it was *he* who was, to the singer's mind, a mere boy Friday. Ellen was at the producer's desk because Dylan was singing these songs just for *her*. And it shows in the performances. Never one for introductions, Dylan felt not the slightest need to explain her presence to mere technicians.

Instead, without any respite, he is off again, tearing into 'Up To Me' before pulling up short, retuning the guitar, and electing to try and (re)capture 'You're A Big Girl Now'. It was not the only time that week he would change songs in midstream. As Ramone archly observed, 'He would almost make a medley of [the songs]. He'd go into [a] second song sometimes, and maybe a third, then come back to the first.'

However, this time he doesn't pull it off. This third take of 'Big Girl' doesn't work, and he knows it. He can feel himself being pulled away from its emotional core by some mysterious centrifugal force. (Of course, in isolation it still sounds effortless, but ain't that so often the case?)

After reminding himself to keep trusting his instincts, he rips into a still-frenetic 'Up To Me', and this time he makes it all the way through. The first of two word-rich epics he set himself the task of recording consecutively, 'Up To Me' was a song for which he had the basic idea early, but did not turn into a song until relatively late in the nine-month process of writing songs for the album.[13]

Indeed, it seems to be another song which only came to life on the farm, prompted by a short narrative Dylan penned at the end of the second working notebook about a postal clerk who falls for a postal customer, only for their paths to cross again at a corner café where she 'sat at a table of men philosophers, poets, agents from some place out of the question' – both these elements later appearing in the song:

> The only decent thing I did when I worked as a postal clerk
> Was to haul your picture down off the wall,
> near the cage where I used to work…
> … Dupree came in pimpin' tonight to the Thunderbird café,
> Crystal wanted to talk to him, I had to look the other way.

[13] A series of rhymes Dylan needs for the title-phrase occupy page five of the second working notebook, as follows: be, by degree, free, flee, he, she, good naturedly, naturally, knee, plea, see, sea, we – thus confirming he had yet to acquire a rhyming dictionary. The idea is put on hold.

The prediluvian spark that triggered the song dated back to when the line between 'Idiot Wind' and another spin-off song was blurred enough to include a couplet like, 'Everything has gone from bad to worse, money didn't change a thing/ You still got the same old thoughts and I still feel the same old sting.'

'Up To Me' at this stage remained a part of the conceptual jigsaw. Dispatched in a single complete take, it would remain on the shortlist until the final mixes, having been pulled to master and remixed twice (five days apart). In fact, this version seems to have been under more serious consideration than the more widely known one included on 1985's *Biograph*, recorded at the final New York session.

The fact that he could verbalize such a complex twelve-verse lyric word-perfect in a single take inspired a certain stunned awe in ear-witnesses – as exemplified by Berger's observation, 'Never looked at lyrics, knew them all!' He was just warming up. The fifth and final song he recorded solo in a little under two hours was a ten-minute traditional-style ballad set in a classic western setting, the gambling saloon.

'Lily, Rosemary And The Jack Of Hearts' was a long song even by Dylan's standards, so when he blew the first take, three and a half minutes and six verses in, he feared the worst. He asked Ramone, 'Can you start the tape over?' suggesting he wanted this failure to be erased from history – as it almost was.[14]

He begins again from the beginning, telling no one in particular, almost off-mike, '[Hope] I'm gonna get through this one.' And get through it, he does – faultlessly. By now, he doesn't just *know* the words, they have become a part of him. He just needs to let his muse reign:

Ellen Bernstein: Bob lived these words as he created them. Most of the tracks grew and changed organically throughout the days we spent in Minnesota. He was totally and completely immersed in the creation of this album, and if that's where you're coming from as a writer and artist, I think it's not a matter of remembering the words because he was living the creation of it and it was a part of him in every way imaginable. It flowed through him. He never needed to look at that little red notebook when he was recording a track. By that

[14] That false start was seemingly erased from the multitrack, and as such omitted by Michael Krogsgaard from his sessionography. The mono reel has preserved it.

time he had absorbed the words as being the way he wanted them, so it never occurred to me that he wouldn't be able to remember them.

Dylan clearly saw the song as another of the album's centrepieces. Placed first in the 'fair copy' notebook he began in Loretto, it appears in the working notebooks between 'Simple Twist Of Fate', a 'final' rewrite of 'Tangled Up In Blue' and 'Shelter From The Storm', where it occupies no fewer than a dozen pages, evidently written largely – if not entirely – while staying at Ellen's, in the original prospector town on the bay.

In the process, Dylan shed a number of Tarot-esque characters – 'the Queen and the King and the Ace in the Hole' – honing the story until the song had been thoroughly revamped, while losing a more threatening opening couplet:

The festival was over and the tables had been turned,
Everything without any purpose had been burned.

What was left was a stalwart performance, where the listener could imagine him 'sittin' in a room singing', a true troubadour. The attention to detail is everywhere, down to the use of 'penknife' as the murder instrument – not the modern penknife but the dagger-like instrument that ubiquitously featured in ancient British ballads.

If writing 'Lily, Rosemary And The Jack Of Hearts' in a matter of days was an extraordinary achievement, dispatching it in a single full take stands comparison. Like the quartet before it, it was pulled to master, becoming the only song recorded that afternoon to make the 'New York' test pressing. Indeed, Dylan would not return to the song again until he made his debatable decision to apply some western swing to it in a Midwest studio at winter's end.

Barely had he finished recording this fifth solo reverie when banjo player/bandleader Eric Weissberg entered the studio and exchanged greetings with his old friend, whom he had first met in Madison, Wisconsin, in December 1960, when the young Dylan was on his way to New York. It had been a while, Weissberg having last 'seen Bob on the street about a year [earlier]. We talked for a while and he said he wanted me to work with him, then I hadn't heard from him.' Now here he was.

★★★

I [just] happened to be home at two in the afternoon ... and the phone rang and a woman says, 'Hi, can you be at Bob's session at 4pm ... Studio A.' I said there's only about 1400 Studio As in New York ... Then it dawned on me it was Columbia's studio.

—Eric Weissberg, October 1974.

Immediately sensing something funny going on, Weissberg later recalled how 'intense' this new Dylan appeared: '[He] seemed a bit ill at ease in the studio, as though he wanted to get it over with.'

The banjo man himself was not there just to say hello, having been summoned to lend a hand and bring his band, the aptly-named Deliverance. As always with Dylan it had all been rather last-minute as he belatedly decided it might be fun to record a few songs with (elements of) a band, à la *John Wesley Harding*. When Weissberg had called back to find out what instruments he should bring, it was Ramone who answered the phone:

Eric Weissberg: I ... asked him who [else] he got. He said he tried everyone but it was too short notice ... So I said I got a band. Just then Bobby walked into the studio and Phil asked Bob and he said, 'Sure, bring the whole band over.' [1974]

Weissberg, an ex-member of the Greenbriar Boys and an ex-boyfriend of Carla Rotolo, had been riding a wave of popularity not entirely his own since January 1973, when his version of 'Dueling Banjos' 45 had hit number two on the *Billboard* charts on the back of its spooky appearance in the film *Deliverance.*

While a lawsuit by its true author, Arthur 'Guitar Boogie' Smith – who composed the song under the title 'Feudin' Banjos' in 1954 – continued looming, Weissberg assembled a band called Deliverance and toured prodigiously.[15] The other four band members – guitarist Charlie Brown III, bassist Tony Brown, drummer Richard Crooks and keyboardist Tom McFaul – now found themselves summoned to A & R. For what purpose, no one knew.

---

[15] Weissberg would lose the suit, which resulted in substantial damages and required the studio to reshoot the film credits to give Smith his due.

Even Dylan didn't seem to know, though he clearly had some kind of musical accompaniment in mind for some of the songs.[16] According to Ramone, it had always been part of the plan: 'Earlier that day, Hammond [had] called and asked if I could line up a few musicians ... Bob [had] decided that he wanted a few extra players.'

Don DeVito had now been dispatched to track down a mandolin player, Dylan having presumably decided that, even after lessons with Grisman, he had yet to reach the requisite standard. The person the A&R man had gone in search of had known their mutual acquaintance since 1961, days when he gave the young pretender an occasional lift to go see his hero, Woody:

Barry Kornfeld: Don DeVito's job then was to 'baby' Bob Dylan. He [knew me when] I was an A&R producer at Epic. For some reason Dylan was doing this album [on the hoof]. It's already the night and I'm teaching at [the] Guitar Study Center. DeVito comes into the class and says, 'Grab your mandolin.' [But] what I had was a metal body, National mandolin. I said, 'This is not [really a mandolin!]' 'Never mind, just bring it.' He actually came to the school, drove me down to my apartment and grabbed a couple of instruments and we took off.

When Kornfeld got to the studio and spoke to Dylan, he phoned mutual acquaintance Steve Wilson, an ex-roommate of Paul Clayton and Village habitué, to inform him, 'Bob is trying to recapture the feeling of yesteryear and he'd like some of the old crowd at the session.' Wilson took this as his cue to hotfoot it to A & R, where it was now getting mighty crowded.

Ramone was probably unaware of Dylan's rather limited experience of working with preexisting bands in the studio. None of his sixties sessions with other combos had been overly successful. His first such attempt – at Levy's in London on May 12th, 1965 – came after he consciously summoned fabled British blues combo, John Mayall's Bluesbreakers. It ended with Mayall caustically commenting, 'You haven't worked much with bands, have you?'

[16] Of the four songs recorded with Deliverance in New York, not one duplicates the five recorded in Minneapolis, suggesting Dylan never really settled on which of these songs suited a band.

Post-*Highway 61* sessions with the Hawks from October and November 1965 and January 1966 fared little better, producing just two tracks deemed releasable at the time (from five days' and nights' toil).

Even the *Planet Waves* sessions, the previous November – which had reunited Dylan with The Band in the studio for the first time since 1966 – were rocky enough for Dylan to attempt two songs solo, after Band versions of 'Wedding Song' and 'Forever Young' left him underwhelmed.[17]

According to *Rolling Stone*'s November report, what happened once Weissberg delivered his band to A & R was that, 'Dylan, [who] had been recording alone for a few hours, … played back those songs, but … wanted to do some new ones, and Deliverance was forced to pick up the tunes cold.'

In fact, Dylan initially wanted to see if Deliverance could bring something extra to the most perfectly realised of the five songs already captured, 'Simple Twist Of Fate'. Yet even this relatively straightforward composition left the bandleader scratching his head:

Eric Weissberg: This is how it got started. Bob came into A & R Studio A-1 and immediately called us to the center of the room, where he began playing and singing [for] the first time. We scrambled for paper and pencils to try and scribble down the changes and the road map, &c. I don't know which song it was, but it had a lot of verses [sic], and we each got our own chart scratched out. Then I think we ran it down once, maybe twice, and Bob asked Phil if he was ready to record … We did our first take. Bob asked for a playback … During the playback, Bob called us to gather around him again and started to run down the next song.

Part of the problem might have been the studio set-up. According to Berger, once he knew who was coming in, the engineer had 'set up the microphones for the band: drums, bass, guitars, keyboard. I put Dylan's mics in the middle of the room, surrounded by [all] these players.' But according to the Deliverance guitarist, the initial set-up isolated the drummer – as was the norm in 1974 – making it almost impossible for Crooks to follow Dylan:

[17] 'Dirge', on the other hand, began life as a solo guitar piece and ended up with Dylan at the piano and Robertson noodling away on guitar.

Charlie Brown III: They had a live set-up for Bob, with a guitar microphone and a vocal microphone there in the room, and all the other guitar players and Tom McFaul, the organist, we were all right there behind him in the room. [But] they took Richard Crooks and put him in a drum booth. Now, in order to hear Richard, you've got to wear your headphones and Bob didn't want to wear headphones. So … you have to put Bob's guitar way up in the phones and simply follow him, which was not that easy, because he tends to shift tempos with his lyrics.

That first taped take of 'Simple Twist Of Fate' seems to bear Brown out. The drums cope well enough with the verses, but when cut adrift from Dylan's vocal anchor, lose their way. A delightful clash of guitars offsets Dylan's singing, but the minute they have to contend with a lagging beat, all is lost, and during an extended harmonica-driven coda Crooks loses the beat completely until the take peters out.

It prompts Ramone to reassuringly remark, 'It's gonna be all right.' But a second take never even gets off the ground before Dylan cuts it short, muttering that 'the drums are one second behind'. As a man who likes his drummer to be on (or even fractionally ahead) of the beat, he is finding the effect a little off-putting.

A third take is a little more filled in, Dylan bending his notes and riding the guitar fills with aplomb, perhaps because, as Charlie Brown III has suggested, 'Richard eventually just kick[ed] the damn door open, or something like that, so we could hear him in the room.' Unfortunately, Dylan's three-strikes-and-out policy means his own boredom threshold has been reached before the band have hit a home run. Time to try something else.

Richard Crooks: He'll do one take of one song, then just move on to another song, and maybe an hour or two later he'll come back and do that first song again, just so you don't lock in on it too much. He likes that loose, unpredictable feel.

If Crooks understood where Dylan was coming from, the experience was proving daunting for some of the others, who were being challenged like never before. Their bandleader was growing increasingly vexed, even as he kept any underlying annoyance to himself at Dylan's failure to explain anything – in particular his unusual tuning:

Eric Weissberg: You couldn't really watch his fingers 'cause he was playing in a tuning arrangement I had never seen before. If it was anybody else I would have walked out. [1974]

It was the Bloomfield tutorial all over again, and it prompted the Deliverance keyboardist to share his boss's burgeoning ire:

Tom McFaul: I think we all felt we were extremely limited in what we could contribute because of the weird recording set-up. Under normal circumstances, this [lack of any] cue … would not be tolerated by the players. But no one said anything.

Yet guitarist Charlie Brown III couldn't help but admire Dylan for sticking to his guns, telling Larry Sloman, weeks later, that Dylan's 'whole concept of making an album seemed to be to go ahead and play it, and whichever way it comes out, well, that's the way it is. It's what happens of the moment … We'd just [have to] watch his hands and pray we had the right changes.' But initially, even Brown was non-plussed:

Charlie Brown III: He didn't use any charts. I finally wound up getting a yellow legal pad and scribbling down a couple of things, which were gone, instantly, right out the window. It wasn't worth bothering to write them down, he changed things so much … Because he wanted the immediacy of the moment – he didn't care whether there were mistakes in there or not; that's just the way it happened … I didn't get the message until about three-quarters of the way through the first day, and then I thought, 'Oh, I know what he's doing. He just wants to hear whatever comes out.'

Sat at the console throughout the ensemble experiment, Ellen knew enough not to interfere, rather letting Deliverance sink or swim, adapt or die. She knew Dylan would keep faith with his own instincts and, nine times out of ten, he would be right.

Ellen Bernstein: He knew as soon as he heard something whether or not it was what he was going for. It never took him more than one time to know … He worked so instinctively, more so than anyone I've ever worked with. The energy level was so high at all times because it wasn't like where you went over and over and over something until all the raw emotion is gone ... It was all very immediate – and very emotional.

As if to prove Ellen's point, after Dylan abandoned 'Simple Twist', he decided to see if Deliverance would fare better with a dose of the blues. It was Bluesbreakers time again. The only question was: *which* blues song to record? He had a few in the 'fair copy' notebook he had tucked away in his pocket, of which the two likeliest contenders were 'Belltower Blues' ('Climbed upon the bell tower ... I couldn't find you anywhere') and 'Church Bell Blues'.

Starting to make selection choices based on what he thought the band could follow, Dylan decided to test the water before wading in. They would run down that straightforward twelve-bar, 'Church Bell Blues', which Dylan now renamed 'Call Letter Blues' (presumably a gesture of respect to Luke Jordan, whose 1927 blues classic laid prior claim to the title).[18]

Still hoping to hear the musicians' first instincts, he was meeting resistance at every turn. The keyboard player was one of those who expected an explanation for every decision and a rehearsal before they ever ran tape. He soon found out he was getting neither:

Tom McFaul: We would record before we had run down a song even once ... I would go up to the piano to find out what key he was in. Dylan would stop me, 'We don't want the piano, we want the organ.' 'I know,' I would say, 'I'm just trying to figure out what key we are ...' 'We don't want the piano, we want the organ.' Yes, sir! I would go back to the B-3, which was ... on the other side of the studio, and which I could not hear, and hope like hell we were in A minor.

Thankfully, for a song like 'Call Letter Blues' any keyboard player was going to be a bystander. Bottleneck blues became the order of the day. For guitarists Weissberg and Brown, it was a chance to show their chops, one they embraced.

---

[18] He would do something similar when he changed 'Danville Girl' – formerly a Guthrie song title – to 'Brownsville Girl' in time for *Knocked Out Loaded*.

Dylan seemed to like the vibe, and immediately began what Ramone calls out as 'take two'. The only indication this isn't 'Call Letter Blues' is the singer belatedly mumbling, 'Let's try this one.' He has switched to another bluesy paradigm, 'Meet Me In The Morning', without telegraphing his intentions, as the band held on for dear life:

Richard Crooks: We'd record a song one way; then he'd say, 'Let's just do another take,' and you'd think you knew where everything was, and all of a sudden the second take would be a little different from the one we'd done before.

Between the farm and the studio, Dylan has reworked an image from the blues lexicon first found in a verse on page one of the second 'working' notebook, only to then disappear from its remaining pages:

My grandfather had a farm, but all he ever raised was the dead,
He had the keys to the kingdom but all he ever opened was his head,
Meet me in the morning, it's the brightest day you ever saw,
We could be in Kansas by the time the snow begins to thaw.

'Meet Me In The Morning' may soon have settled into the same groove as 'Call Letter', but it comes from an entirely different place. This time Deliverance have learnt to embrace Dylan's 'wing it' methodology, making at least one musician radically revise his opinion of the frontman:

Richard Crooks: I [had] never thought of Dylan as much of a musician, but … this guy was unbelievable. As well as having a phenomenal memory for lyrics, he had a [really] good grasp of musical technique. He would say, 'Ah, I don't like it in that key,' and change to another, but he never capo'd anything on the guitar. He would barre-chord the changes. We probably went through six or seven different keys on just one song, and he never capo'd anything. He had all the transpositions right there, bang, bang, bang … If you listen to some of the stuff he does, it's very simple in terms of the playing and chord structures. But he could do anything he wanted.

Having taken Deliverance into the swamplands of southern blues, Dylan laid down the album's one full-on electric excursion in a single take, then returned to 'Call Letter Blues', the spirit of 'Meet Me In The Morning' having now seeped into its blue bones. Combining the slightly sloppy downhome feel of take one with the *braggadocio* of 'Meet Me In The Morning', this 'take three' [sic] later made its way onto 1991's *Bootleg Series 1-3*. It also laid bare the situation in his marriage with the couplet, 'Well, children cry for mother/ I tell them, mother took a trip.'

Such searing honesty probably explains its omission from the artifact, though it got as far as being pulled to master, overdubbed and mixed while Dylan continued baring his soul nightly.

Neither blues song would ever be attempted again – in studio or on stage![19] For Deliverance, it was a relief to find they were being asked to take a breather and regroup, just as another musician arrived to lend a helping hand. (Or not.) The arrivee found a surprisingly uptight Dylan awaiting him:

Barry Kornfeld: As I recall, Bobby was recording 'Idiot Wind' – not his best work … Dylan was not in his best form as a person at that time. He was one-upping a lot. He told a joke I don't remember, and one of us laughed. He said, 'You think that's funny?' He was a much more fun cat in the early days … We never did find out what it was that I was supposed to do.

If Kornfeld did little to earn his AFM fee, bass player Tony Brown was being made to work double-hard for his. He – and he alone – was now asked to fill in the sound on another of the album's centrepieces, 'Idiot Wind'.

Dylan was replaying a past trick, one he'd adopted at the January 1973 Mexico City *Pat Garrett & Billy The Kid* session, when he requisitioned Terry Paul to record a guitar/bass version of the 'Billy' ballad when band versions were just not working. For Brown, this was both a dream come true and a potential

---

[19] *Rolling Stone* reported at the time that 'Meet Me In The Morning' was attempted in Minneapolis but this was not the case. The one time 'Meet Me In The Morning' was ostensibly attempted live, in 2007, it was left to guest Jack Black to take the lead, Dylan resisting every attempt at a duet.

nightmare, having kept from Dylan just how huge a fan of his work he had always been:

Tony Brown: Coming from a very left-wing family, I was raised on folk music: The Weavers, Pete Seeger, Odetta, Woody Guthrie, Leadbelly, etc. So ... I became familiar with Dylan early on; first album we bought was *Freewheelin'*. From then on, I'd be buying his records as soon as they were released. [I] also saw him play live a few times, including the great Philharmonic Hall [Halloween 1964] concert and the infamous Forest Hills [August 1965] gig.

A mighty nervous Brown knew Dylan was impatient to start, but expected a little more understanding from A & R's chief engineer when requesting a little break in order to 'write these charts down'. It was gonna be a long song and, with just him and Bob, there would be no place to hide. Instead, producer Phil flatly disabused him, 'He won't do it the same way twice,' Ramonespeak for, You're wasting your time.

The bassist turned to the assistant engineer for help. Berger suggested a solution of sorts – proximity – so 'he sat inches from Dylan, watching his hands, trying to follow the chord changes as Bob made them, never knowing what chord or song was to come in the next moment. This was especially hard ... because Dylan was playing in an "open" tuning.'

It was always going to be a monumental task capturing the right tone quickly on a song with perhaps the most complex compositional history in Dylan's kaleidoscopic career. Lyrics which began as a patchwork of recrimination and remorse months earlier had been woven and rewoven, with multiple additions and excisions, as Dylan first repented of his lowdown ways and then lashed out at the public image he could never escape.

Perhaps the defining moment in the song's genesis came at the end of June, when he read a juicy snippet from syndicated gossipmonger Earl Wilson, whose June 22nd column reported: 'Bob Dylan and wife Sara (parents of five) [have] separated. He is friendly with Laurie [sic] Sebastian, ex-wife of John Sebastian of The Lovin' Spoonful.'

The story apparently even made it to the CBS-TV news and, in early July, *Rolling Stone*, prompting a swift rebuttal from an incensed Lorey, who denied any involvement with Dylan. An unconcerned Wilson had managed three major factual errors in the space of a single sentence, inspiring the same Dylan who had written 'Restless Farewell' back in October 1963 – after *Newsweek*'s Andrea Svedburg attempted to cover him in her 'dust of rumors' – to reveal himself again.

By September 16th, 1974, all that remained of his riposte to Wilson specifically – and gossipmongers in general – was 'Idiot Wind's introductory line. But, oh, what an opening volley: 'Someone's got it in for me, they're planting stories in the press.'

It was the last vestige of an extensive insert into an already well-advanced 'Idiot Wind'. Appearing halfway through the second working notebook, it has all the immediacy of something personal, to which Dylan is responding in real time. The original riposte includes lines both funnier and more revealing than the *Gatsby*-esque, 'They say I shot a man named Gray':

> Well now, there's a story floating around
> That I made it with a camel late last week
> Someplace in Jerusalem.

If these lines went by the board completely, other couplets were ultimately changed from the third-person to a more accusatory second-person singular, viz., 'Even she asked me if it was true/ I just couldn't believe, after all these years, she didn't know me any better than that.'

If this was written in the immediate aftermath of the Wilson story – as it surely was – Dylan had been playing around with this momentous song for close to six months. The same sheet as the 'Tour '74' 'Big Girl Now' draft includes a passing reference to a song called 'Idiot Wind' and the cryptic phrase, 'shake your head/ change your ways'.

Meanwhile, on page six of the first notebook – which contains fragments of all three 'trigger' songs, 'Tangled', 'Simple Twist' and 'Idiot Wind' – we find his first attempt to find a partner-image for the Grand Coulee Dam and a couplet still hinting at reconciliation:

> Now you play for pennies and dance for kings
> When the curtain falls, I'll still be waiting in the wings.

By the third page of the crammed-to-the-brim second working notebook, Dylan has 'buttons of our coats/ letter that we wrote'. Throughout the remainder of this notebook, he returns again and again to what he already sees as one of the album's defining songs. A decade later he revealed, in conversation with *Musician*'s Bill Flanagan, what drove him to constantly reinvent the song:

Bob Dylan: [I] changed some of it … I [just] thought that it seemed so personal that people would think it was about so-and-so, who was close to me … 'Cause usually with those kinds of things, if you think you're too close to something, you're giving away too much of your feelings. Well, your feelings are going to change a month later and you're going to look back and say, 'What did I do that for?'

Knowing that the last thing he needed was a 'Ballad In Plain D' for the seventies, he kept chipping away, obfuscating with rich symbolism, adding layers of meaning at the expense of an unvarnished account of the end of a marriage. Even when he makes a fair copy in the Loretto notebook, he can't let it be, imposing two more major rewrites on 'Idiot Wind' in the last few pages.

As such, it should come as no great surprise that 'Idiot Wind' on that first night at A & R should be the one song where Dylan would attempt to change the odd line, going from 'bad ideas, images and recorded facts' on take one to 'false ideas, images and distorted facts' by take two.[20] Fatally, he trips over the words, not once but three times on separate takes, much to his audible exasperation. As a result, he would come close to giving up.

Unfortunately for Dylan, take three is particularly magnificent – perhaps the best of the lot – until he reaches the final verse and it all comes crashing down – proving to be Dylan's 'In The Ghetto'.[21] He

[20] Berger has noted how 'Dylan just left a yellow pad with lyrics scribbled on it on the piano and I didn't take it. It looked like he was taking dictation as he wrote. No hesitation at all. As I'm sure he's done endlessly, he'd do different lyrics on different takes.' Yet the only major lyrical changes at the sessions were verses cut from 'Meet Me In The Morning' and 'Shelter From The Storm'.

[21] Presley blew a near-perfect version of said song at the end of take one during the fabled 1969 American Studio sessions and never quite got back there, in the end using the eleventh take. Its author, Mac Davis, would meet both Ellen and Dylan at a private party in the summertime of '74. (See photo on page 3.)

does not even try to hide his disappointment, 'Ah, we got to go all the way back – son of a bitch!'

Yet even Ramone can't convince Dylan to punch in a line or two, or keep going when he stumbles over a single word or the bassist fluffs a change, something he alleges happened repeatedly, '[When] Dylan moved his hands to another chord suddenly, the bass part would be wrong at that point ... [However,] I never stopped a take.'

What Dylan *is* prepared to do – so convinced is he of the merits of this third take – is record an insert of the final verse for perhaps the first time since 'I Shall Be Free #10' in June 1964. When he fails to get even this right, he lets fly, 'Oh, I really fucked it up.'

At least doing a handful of takes allows Brown to figure out his part. And so when Dylan steels himself to get through the whole thing one damn time, come what may, he holds his own. Finally, on take 'six' they capture the song whole, after the briefest of false starts (take five).[22]

If Dylan duly delivers an eight-minute 'Idiot Wind' that wrestles with every emotion, it is not entirely convincing. Yet take six will be deemed good enough to make the final shortlist – a straight shoot-off with another guitar/bass version from three days later. And even when it loses that duel, it will be used by *Bootleg Series 1-3*'s producer Jeff Rosen, who preferred to include something starker and, crucially, unbootlegged.

Dylan is not done for the day, though, and nor are Deliverance. He wants his money's worth, instituting the most tortuous part of that evening's protracted proceedings: trying to teach Weissberg and co. 'You're Gonna Make Me Lonesome When You Go'.

The first song he entered in the second working notebook, and probably the second song (after 'Big Girl Now') completed to Dylan's satisfaction, 'You're Gonna Make Me Lonesome When You Go' may be another song directly inspired by an event in Dylan's life, in this instance the occasion Ellen went on vacation without him to Hawaii.

He apparently feared she might never return, or might do so having changed her mind about continuing an affair with a married man. Such feelings probably prompt him to proclaim in an early

---

[22] I know not where take four has gone, but presumably it was erased. The insert is marked 3A. The revelation revealed by the Minneapolis multitracks that the vocal on the released 'Idiot Wind' is an overdub rather makes one wonder what stopped Dylan three months earlier from doing the same, or splicing takes three and six together, as he would do with the 'Hurricane' 45.

draft, 'This time I feel no remorse.' Having promised his wife he can change, he proceeds to tell this year's model: 'I've changed ever since you said hello.'

Despite the affectionate nature of the song, a bittersweet residue lingers throughout the various drafts, as if the narrator knows this is only a holding station and it must end. Indeed, a song he begins to write simultaneously, 'You Were Good To Me', which will end up donating a few lines to 'You're Gonna Make Me Lonesome', places such a relationship in the past tense (while the chorus includes the telling admission, 'I been too long without a wife').

For all that, 'You're Gonna Make Me Lonesome' provides some much-needed relief from self-recrimination. It also lent itself to an upbeat soft-shoe shuffle, the likes of which a band like Deliverance could play in their sleep.

Once again, though, Deliverance fail the audition, thanks in no small part to Dylan's insistence that they record without (him) wearing headphones. For once, Weissberg is prompted to voice his dissatisfaction on tape after the song breaks down twice within a couple of minutes of Dylan kicking off take one with some effective harmonica.

A perplexed Dylan, who without phones cannot really hear the drums, asks, 'What's the matter?' Ramone informs him, 'It was getting out of time,' prompting Weissberg to finally say something captured by the mono reference reel, 'Since Bob's not wearing phones, I don't know what we should have in ours. 'Cause it's hard for us to hear *him*, we're getting out of meter.' Ramone suggests the problem is 'more … the drums', but it is Dylan's Luddite ways which are making it difficult for everyone (else):

Glenn Berger: If any of the musicians, trying to keep up with [some] unexpected switch, missed a chord, he'd wave his hand, signaling them to drop out … This was Dylan. No one would tell him he couldn't do this. But … you are at least supposed to tell the musicians the key and the song. Everyone there had been incredibly excited to be playing with this guy, making a record with him … but it was becoming apparent to each musician, as they were summarily dismissed, that this was not likely to happen … We all stole looks at each other, not understanding what was going on, not knowing what to do … This hurt. You could see it in the musicians' eyes, as they sat silently behind their instruments, forced not to play by the mercurial whim of the guy painting his masterpiece.

Ramone's attitude wasn't helping either. He again failed to endear himself to a set of musicians he would need soon enough. According to Charlie Brown III, 'We would go in [to the console room] ... asking him, 'Can you get Bob to do this?' Whatever it was ... Ramone never opened his mouth, never [even] responded. It drove me crazy.' McFaul cited one specific instance where he 'heard the assistant engineer whisper to Phil that the snare drum mike was not working. Phil just waved him off.'

Ramone already knew better than to question Dylan. On the one occasion when someone did offer advice in the studio, Crooks remembers Dylan snapping back, 'Y'know, if I'd listened to everybody who told me how to do stuff, I might be somewhere by now.' The surefooted Dylan of old was back, and he was calling the shots, not Ramone. Alienating the artist was not on the cards.

After another stuttering third take, it is Dylan who audibly asserts, 'It seems a little heavy,' and who comes up with a potential solution – lose the drums and record the song with just guitars and organ. Now, for the first time that evening, McFaul makes his presence felt as Dylan asks for 'more organ – like a church choir'. They almost make it all the way this time, too. But Dylan knows it's not right.

Perhaps he just needs to slow it down. Slow it down he does, reintroducing Crooks into the mix for a torch-ballad take that goes all the way, putting an entirely different spin on the song, amplifying the sense of imminent loss even before an extended harmonica coda stretches its melancholic mood to breaking point.

More of a piece with the rest of the released album, this take five of 'You're Gonna Make Me Lonesome' never even makes the following night's 'pulled to master' reels, for a simple reason – they weren't rolling multitrack tape. Or if they were, they erased it, along with three other takes of the song:

Charlie Brown III: Every time we'd go into the booth to listen back to it ... either he'd say, I don't like that, or there's something wrong with it. I think he was generally referring to his own performance, because he would say, 'Erase that.'

It seems Dylan really did take the view that it was better to record and lose the tape than never to have recorded at all. His dissatisfaction with how it was going was now doing a disservice to posterity.[23] Thankfully, take eight not only resembled a sprightly country cousin of 'New Morning' but this time everyone made the finishing line in tandem. It would be the band's last delivery of the evening.

Yet there was at least one more song Dylan and Deliverance had worked on. Back before the first false start on 'You're Gonna Make Me Lonesome', Ramone is uncertain as to which song they are planning to record and asks Dylan, 'Is this the first one we ran down?' Evidently, they rehearsed more than one song *before rolling tape.*

The studio sheet suggests a name for the other song. 'You're A Big Girl Now' 'w/ band' is written at the top of the studio log, then crossed out. Seemingly lost for good, the Deliverance arrangement of 'You're A Big Girl Now' was abandoned by Dylan before the eight takes of 'Lonesome'.

He was rapidly becoming convinced that the album for which he had already recorded eight songs would be light on embellishment, and his most acoustic-sounding record in a decade.[24] However, he is *still* not done for the evening. He wants to record one more song.

Whether the other members of Deliverance hung around is undocumented but the hour is getting late as it was Brown's turn to shine again. Saving the best for last, Dylan wanted to cut the moving ballad which had unblocked an eight-year creative dam, through which all of *Blood On The Tracks* subsequently flowed.

When Dylan began his *Planet Waves* sleeve notes with the line, 'Back to the starting point', he was probably already looking to write a song like 'Tangled Up In Blue'. Indeed, he may already have begun fumbling for the switch to that inner lightbulb in the days before penning those notes, which appear on page one of his personal tour diary.

What he didn't appear to have taken with him on the road was a five-inch red notebook he will use sporadically between late October 1973 and October 1974. In it were just twenty-six pages of jotted down notes, song ideas and book titles.

---

[23] If they did preserve takes four to seven on multitrack, the tapes have been mislaid. Only the mono reference reel/s – thankfully – remain.

[24] It could be argued that the Sound 80 'Big Girl Now' suggests an electric version was never a good idea, but exemplary electric interpretations in 1976, 1978 and 1988 suggest otherwise.

It also included on page one a shorthand version of the 'he was always in a hurry, too busy or too stoned' verse to 'Tangled Up In Blue', so it's probable he began the song pre-tour. Two pages later, 'She [has] moved in a little bit closer/ And studied the lines on my face', and by page seventeen he has arrived at Montague Street, where 'we listened a lot to Coltrane', though 'the revolution never came'.

The framework was thus in place for 'Tangled Up In Blue' even before he splurged out for a blue replacement notebook – having presumably left the red one behind in Malibu, from where it was rescued in time to include a list of three books published in October 1974.

Dylan was soon hard at work on the songs this tangled tale has triggered – notably 'Simple Twist Of Fate' and 'Idiot Wind' – filling each crevice of wood pulp every which way. Yet 'Tangled' does not re-emerge till page 25 when – without a definitive title or a refrain – he writes down sixteen rhymes for 'blue' – *jew, who, few, clue, do, flew, grew, new, rue, sue, too, you, zoo, shoe, glue, view*; plus the telling line, 'Some seek happiness, others seek revenge.'

By page 45 – when he appears to have been in San Francisco with Ellen – he was calling it 'Dusty Sweatbox Blues' (I kid you not). He had the opening verse almost down, but he still did not write out a clean text; or if he did, it was the one he inserted into the 'fair copy' notebook immediately after 'Lily, Rosemary And The Jack Of Hearts' – also written down by the bay.

That version in the 'fair copy' notebook is pretty much the song Dylan chooses to record to bookend his first day at A & R. Once again, he has asked a petrified Tony Brown to ride his coattails, the only thought running now through Brown's head being, Remember *John Wesley Harding*:

Tony Brown: I loved that album and the way that Charlie McCoy was wholly in sync with him. [So] that was in mind throughout. Because it was hard, working with Dylan. He doesn't say a thing – not a goddamn thing.

Remarkably, Dylan's lack of guidance worked a charm. He and Brown cut the song in a single take, with a little help from an unattributed second guitarist, who is not Barry Kornfeld, who continued sitting around getting paid scale to see genius at work. (Contrary to 1991 album credits, neither is this the version released on *Bootleg Series 1-3*, a set which also assigns other inaudible guitarists to the strictly solo 'If You See Her, Say Hello'.)

Again, though, Dylan was just testing the water – and the bassist. He knew 'Tangled Up In Blue' was a song he needed to get just right, having surely already pencilled it in as the album opener. Unbeknownst to the blue bassist trudging home, convinced the day had not 'gone well', he would get plenty more chances to prove his musical mettle in the days ahead. Dylan may have kept his feelings to himself, but he liked what he heard Brown playing throughout an extraordinary evening that left an assistant engineer simply awestruck:

Glenn Berger: We [had] cut the entire album in one day like that. Now that blew my mind. I was nineteen years old and trying to learn how to make art. The style of the time was set by guys I was working with like Paul Simon, who would take weeks recording a guitar part only to throw it away.

Here was the key difference between Dylan and Paul Simon in the studio. The former never raked over a song till the last ember inside died. The latter would happily spend a hundred hours-plus getting 'The Boxer' and still have it come out sounding like a demo.

Despite being at odds with his chosen band most of the time, Dylan had the takes of 'Meet Me In The Morning' and 'Call Letter Blues' he wanted, and had captured releasable takes of some seven other songs, two with Brown and the five he had cut solo when 'killing time' waiting on the band.

The decision to run mono reference reels in tandem with the multis had even ensured that the rather moving 'slow' electric version of 'You're Gonna Make Me Lonesome When You Go' had not been lost to a whim.[25]

---

[25] Why said tape was ever in mono is still unclear. Just to muddy the water further, the reference tapes from the final session on the 19th are also extant, and are two-track. The reference tapes from the 17th and 18th, if they were ever made, have been lost. Berger confirms that they usually did run a reference-tape at A & R sessions and that it was usually a two-track 'live mix' – at 15 ips. Yet two of the three 'ref.' reels from the 16th were 7½ ips, meaning there was no possibility such tapes could have been used officially in 1974, no matter how great a performance was captured. *The Basement Tapes* had yet to break the mould.

Dylan himself was not thinking about the takes that had fallen by the wayside. By the time he returned to Silverstein's West Village apartment with Ellen in the wee small hours he knew he could enjoy the sleep of the just. If the 1974 CBS would never have countenanced releasing an 'entire album [recorded] in one day', every take from here on was designed to top and tail the work he had done on that first evening.

Of course, this being Dylan, just two of the performances from the epic session on the 16th would make the 'final' New York album: 'Lily, Rosemary And The Jack Of Hearts' and 'Meet Me In The Morning'. It was January 13th, 1965, all over again – the last time he had executed an album's worth of songs solo in a single session, then scrapped every single take and started again. The result then had been *Bringing It All Back Home*, an album for the ages.

For now, he had five solo keepers and raw bass/guitar takes of both epic statements he planned to build the album around – 'Idiot Wind' and 'Tangled Up In Blue' – either of which could have sufficed if subsequent retakes had not passed muster.

His mind was clear, his focus unerring. Tomorrow, he would resume where he had left off, with just bassist Brown *in situ*. The band experiment was at an end – for the duration. These songs were too personal to allow his vision to be diffused by endlessly tutoring others in an aesthetic only he and the girl behind the shades seemed to fully understand.

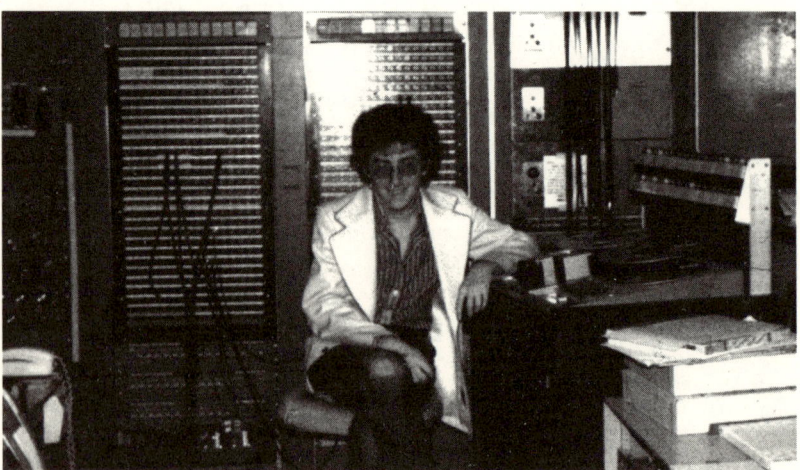

Glenn Berger

(iii)

I got a call the [following] afternoon from a woman, who I believe worked for Columbia, telling me to come in for that evening's session. I remember asking her if she had called Eric about this, and she replied something like, 'No, Bob just wants you.' ... I was almost a bit surprised they called me back, because I did not think the first day had gone well.

—Tony Brown to author.

Brown had not heard the tapes from the first afternoon, so had no idea just how productive the first part of proceedings on the 16th had been, but his 2018 view of the songs on which he did play is that 'the twelve-bar blues songs were decent enough but the other songs, in my view, were of a completely different nature, and I didn't feel as a group we were sensitive enough to give those songs the more nuanced treatment they deserved. It [all] felt too heavy-handed.'

After he 'sat down alone with [Dylan] the next day', Brown quickly realised 'we had attempted a number of those songs at the previous session'. Given the concerns he'd kept to himself, it was presumably no great surprise when the singer expressed a desire to return to a number of songs he'd attempted with and without Deliverance: specifically 'You're A Big Girl Now', rehearsed but not recorded; 'You're Gonna Make Me Lonesome', which certainly required a 'more nuanced treatment'; and 'Tangled Up In Blue', which the pair had almost captured in the midnight hour.

This time around the internal iceberg separating Dylan from his musical sidekick began to thaw, even if his methodology remained unchanged:

Tony Brown: He'd just start playing, I'd listen for a bit and then wing it. He was using an open tuning, so I had to rely on my ear rather than read the chord changes off his hand. [But] unlike the previous day with Deliverance, I was sitting right next to him so I could actually hear his lyrics and voice so that helped me get into it.

Clearly, Dylan saw tonight's session as more a case of tying up loose ends than a brand-new start. In fact, after recently reviewing the studio sheets, Berger was shocked to discover 'I'd pull[ed so many] master takes [from the 16th] the next day ... I guess we thought those were finals until he decided to redo them.'

Dylan was convinced he had the bulk of the album under his belt. He just needed another crack at three or four tracks he hadn't quite got, and two songs he had not yet attempted, one of which – 'Buckets Of Rain' – he may still have been finishing up. Like 'Meet Me In The Morning', it is absent from even the 'fair copy' notebook – save for a scrap of an idea on the final page, 'Little red wagon, little red bike/ I ain't no monkey but I know what I like,' which he then crossed out.

What he hadn't yet abandoned was the idea of adding musical colour to some tracks. Again, he looked to past associations for the right man. Keyboardist Paul Griffin had last played with Dylan in 1966, when he had received an emergency call mid-session to come and salvage 'One Of Us Must Know', after the singer-songwriter's attempts to capture the song with the Hawks had floundered on an inability to communicate his musical ideas in the studio to the band who backed him nightly.

A supremely gifted pianist, Griffin was one of the musicians Tom Wilson had recruited to play on Simon & Garfunkel's first folk-rock album (*Sounds Of Silence*), after Dylan gave his most sympathetic producer the boot. It was an association that continued long after the one enjoyed with Dylan, who may have had to remind himself how great Griffin could be by listening to his contribution to one song on *There Goes Rhymin' Simon,* 'Tenderness'. It certainly seems to have been his idea to summon the piano man and on the evidence of the songs they cut, he greatly enjoyed their musical reunion.

Griffin appears to have already been at A & R when an enthused Brown arrived to resume recording:

Tony Brown: I did not know him but I certainly knew his work. He was an amazing player with an infectious energy as well as an innate sensitivity to the feeling of the song. We cut 'Idiot Wind' [sic] and 'Big Girl Now' live. I believe [pedal steel player] Buddy Cage was also live on 'Big Girl Now', and he, too, was brilliant. I have a pretty clear visual memory of where each of us were sitting in the studio, so I'm quite certain Cage was live.

Clear visual memory or not, it was just Dylan, Brown and Griffin on the 17th. Griffin would later overdub organ on an 'Idiot Wind' recorded at a subsequent session (of which more later), but Brown and Buddy Cage never recorded together.

In fact, Brown was required to sit out a couple of songs on which Dylan wished to play off Griffin alone. But the first song attempted on the 17th was a delightful arrangement of 'You're A Big Girl Now' that featured both Brown and Griffin, flicking that organ on and off. It took just two takes to achieve near-as-dammit perfection, only for pedal steel to be added the next day.

Although Ramone insisted to Odegard, 'I always ran a mix as we were recording, because many times when you go back and try to change the equation, it changes everything,' any reference mix they ran on this evening has been mislaid. So the only way to hear 'You're A Big Girl Now' without that pedal steel overdub would be to remix the one on *Biograph* (itself a remix),[26] or rewind to the first take, which was never overdubbed because it was never under consideration, being more of a rehearsal than a full-blown take.

And yet, as with 'If You See Her, Say Hello' on the opening session, Dylan chooses to warm himself up with an extended harmonica-led coda on take one. This time, though, he has to play off two other musicians, neither of whom is sure how long he intends to keep going. The answer, my friend, is past the five-minute mark.[27]

Dylan knew right away this combination had potential, thus confirming Ellen's assertion, 'It never took him more than one time to know.' It only took one more take to iron out the ending, after which they had a keeper.

Next up was another song which hadn't quite made the grade the night before. This time they got it in a single take, creating the

[26] Griffin's organ has been deliberately mixed down on the 1985 collection compared with how it sounds on the original New York test pressing.

[27] Dylan never did quite figure out how to explain to musicians how to end such songs. On the 1984 rewrite of 'Simple Twist Of Fate', the woefully under-rehearsed musicians were often left hanging in mid-air until drummer Colin Allen finally tackled Dylan about it and was told, 'I just figure we've done enough with the songs and that we should finish … when we feel comfortable.'

first of many mysteries from that second session. Riding the crests of Griffin's vamped waves of sound while Brown attends to the valleys below, Dylan sings the majestic lyrics at a clip, never losing the thread. A joyful harmonica/organ mini-jam at song's end draws whoops of approval from the other side of the glass.

Dylan's decision to ignore this version of 'Tangled Up In Blue' – cut in one resplendent seven-minute take – when pulling takes to master reels at evening's end, is odd even by his standards.

And if Dylan really wasn't happy with what Griffin was bringing to the song, why did he now sideline Brown and record a couple of songs with Griffin alone? Having tested to see if their previous musical telepathy had survived the years, he now decided to see if it could survive the former switching to piano, as he had done on 'Like A Rolling Stone'.[28]

The imperturbable Griffin never loses his cool. He even remains unfazed when Dylan decides to warm up for the change with a spirited but rather off-key version of 'Spanish Is The Loving Tongue'. Griffin plays along, unsure whether Dylan is even rolling tape. He is, though heaven knows why, having already trashed the song beyond repair on the *Dylan* album (from the *Self Portrait* sessions), only to raise it from the dead with his own solo piano version at the *New Morning* sessions.

Perhaps it's Dylan's way of putting himself in the mood for what will be the most exuberant moment of the sessions so far: a roller coaster 'You're Gonna Make Me Lonesome When You Go' that leaves Griffin hanging on to Dylan's neck brace by his pianoforte fingers in a race to the finishing line.

That it was indeed a race – and possibly a photo finish – is confirmed by Ellen, who calls out the time on her stopwatch just as an enthused Dylan asks, 'What's the verdict?' The verdict seems to be that it was a lot of fun, but like as not unsuitable for a slot on the album he had already framed in his made-up mind. He will return to it with just Brown later in the evening, but only after seeing if an equally surreal guitar/piano duel might work better on an important new song, 'Shelter From The Storm'.

One of the few songs written that year which seems to have come

---

[28] Griffin began on organ at the fabled June 16th, 1965, session before moving to piano, leaving Al Kooper to fumble for the light switch.

in one rapid-fire burst of inspiration, 'Shelter' appears first at the end of the second working notebook. Previously, Dylan had been toying around with an idea for a song in which 'cruelty is the message, the crown is one [of] thorns', and getting nowhere. Just when he is about to give up, three lines define an image not of crucifixion but of redemption:

> Suddenly I looked around and she was standing there,
> With silver rings on her fingers and wild flowers in her hair,
> She walked up to me so gracefully and took my crown of thorns.

Over the next two pages, the whole song comes together with what seems like minimal birth pangs. Just one verse gets a vastly superior rewrite. Verse nine originally read thus:

> I been moved out from the factory and stranded in the leaves
> It's a holy sin but a man must pay for everything he believes,
> Poisoned in the bushes and rolled on New Year's Eve
> I was hanging in the distance and ravaged in the corn...

When he starts recording the song on the 17th, he is probably thinking it should be as upbeat as its redemptive ending, perhaps even an album closer. Griffin isn't entirely convinced, and Dylan leaves the experiment permanently on hold after a single spirited, if slightly shambolic, take that includes the extra 'Now the bonds are broken, but they can be retied' verse found in the 'fair copy' notebook.[29] 'Tis now time for Griffin to take a hike. His duties are done, save for a last-minute overdub three weeks later to another track in need of a spark.

Dylan has decided to see if 'Shelter From The Storm' and another new song, 'Buckets Of Rain', would benefit from the same bass/guitar treatment already given 'Idiot Wind' and 'Tangled Up In Blue'. He also thinks 'Tangled Up In Blue' deserves another try.

After 'Buckets Of Rain' fails to find its feet right away, Dylan insists, 'I can do that better.' Just not right away. As Crooks had

---

[29] This was the very take which ended up being licensed for the soundtrack to the 1996 film *Jerry Maguire*, directed by Cameron Crowe, with Griffin mixed out to give the impression of a solo take. In the process, the interplay that explains Dylan's musical choices vanishes. Most peculiar, Mama.

already noticed, he was someone who liked to switch songs, 'so you don't lock in on it too much.' No danger of that. Brown must have been slightly mystified when he called out 'Tangled Up In Blue'. Surely they had already got that one, first in its guitars/bass guise the night before, and then with Griffin applying the odd flick of the wrist, earlier this evening.

Whatever Dylan thought was missing was duly captured on what was third-time-lucky for Brown, as they eased their way into an emotion-filled performance good enough to be pulled to master, but not to be mixed: that is, until 1991 when a line Dylan fluffed on the multitrack – 'She was working in a topless place' – suddenly appeared on a version released on *Bootleg Series 1-3* (misattributed to the 16th).[30]

It would be the start of a productive few hours. All four songs Dylan recorded with Brown during the second half of the evening would be pulled to master reels at session's end, though would go unmixed. If 'Tangled' was very, very close to its core self – one punch-in away, in fact – the second 'Buckets Of Rain' of the evening wasn't quite ready for a remix, though it did not go as off-piste as take one.

No such charge could be levelled at the fourth take of 'Shelter From The Storm', which was pulled to master but only mixed after the final session, Dylan having presumably been reminded just how good it was. The third of three guitar/bass takes, it comes after a second take slows things down from a frenetic first take that dispatches the whole ten verses in under four and a half minutes. When the second, slower take breaks down, Ramone tells Dylan, 'I like that tempo.'

Tempo was also a pressing issue when it came to 'You're Gonna Make Me Lonesome When You Go', though it was one Dylan refrained from resolving. He concludes the second session by re-recording the song in both 'slow' and 'fast' incarnations, pulling both to master, ultimately electing to include the latter to lighten the tone of the album. That take called time on the recording part

---

[30] One must presume the punched-in couplet 'She was working in a topless place/ When I stopped in for a beer' has been taken from the test pressing version. The master reel suggests as much, adding in a later hand, 'new edit of old take – topless bar'. It was not the only such composite on that 1991 set. 'Series Of Dreams' proved to be an edit of two takes.

of the second session, which, according to the AFM sheets, ran till one in the morning.

For Dylan (and Ellen), it was decision time. Which songs to pull to master reels? That was the question. In just two sessions, he had recorded the twelve songs from which he intended to sculpt his new album, before creating three master reels by including two takes each of 'You're A Big Girl Now' (the second solo take from day one and tonight's three-piece version) and 'You're Gonna Make Me Lonesome'; one take each of the other ten. The eight takes from yesterday's marathon session included five afternoon solo performances, while Griffin's contribution this evening was confined to 'You're A Big Girl Now'.

They returned the following evening to start mixing and fixing up what they had. It seemed the heavy lifting had been done in less time than either *Bringing It All Back Home* or *John Wesley Harding*. However, unbeknownst to a delighted Dylan, he was really only at a halfway house when it came to the 'New York' album, and only three songs cut so far would make it all the way to the released artifact.[31] The unmaking had begun.

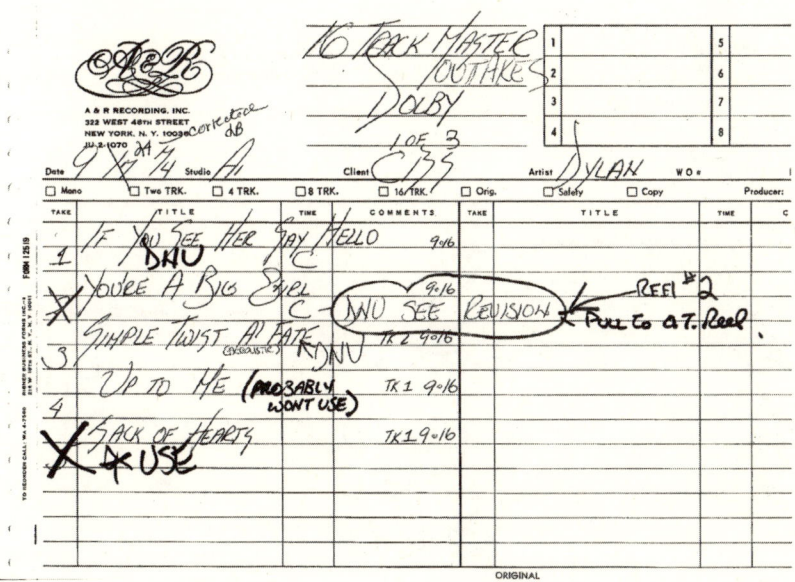

[31] The trio of cuts would comprise the one song with Deliverance that passed muster ('Meet Me In The Morning') and the last two tracks captured with Brown on the 17th.

A & R RECORDING, INC.
322 WEST 48TH STREET
NEW YORK, N. Y. 10036
JU 2-1070

16 TRACK MASTER
O.T.
DOLBY
2 OF 3

Date 9/x/74 2nd corrected dB Studio A1 Client CBS Artist DYLAN WO #

☐ Mono ☐ Two TRK. ☐ 4 TRK. ☐ 8 TRK. ☐ 16 TRK. ☐ Orig. ☐ Safety ☐ Copy Producer:

TAKE	TITLE	TIME	COMMENTS	TAKE	TITLE	TIME	COM
✗	MEET ME IN THE MORNING FAST 3 VERSES EDIT- LAST VERS *USE						
2	CALL LETTER BLUES ∆NU @ ALL						
✗	(IDIOT WIND)						
✗	YOU'RE A BIG GIRL - REVISION **USE						

ORIGINAL

A & R RECORDING, INC.
322 WEST 48TH STREET
NEW YORK, N. Y. 10036
JU 2-1070

16 TRK MASTER
- OUTAKES
3 OF 3

Date 9/24/74 Studio A1 Client CBS Artist DYLAN WO #

☐ Mono ☐ Two TRK. ☐ 4 TRK. ☐ 8 TRK. ☐ 16 TRK. ☐ Orig. ☐ Safety ☐ Copy Producer:

TAKE	TITLE	TIME	COMMENTS	TAKE	TITLE	TIME	C
~~1~~	~~YOU'RE A BIG GIRL (NU)~~						
1	BUCKETS OF RAIN ∆NU				✗→ out to MS 9/17		
✗2	SHELTER @ *USE						
3	LONESOME SLOW *						
3½	LONESOME FAST * ThNEWER USE						
4	TANGLED UP IN BLUE ∆NU See Redo			* WITH NEW EDIT From 1ST TWO Choruses Dubs			

ORIGINAL

★★★

By the next afternoon, Dylan was not so sure of himself and all he had wrought. As they began to mix songs from the master reels, a few takes fell foul of the review process, perhaps reflecting a darker mood on Dylan's part.

In the end, Dylan chose to let Ramone mix just eight songs: 'Simple Twist Of Fate', 'Up To Me', 'Lily, Rosemary And The Jack Of Hearts', 'Meet Me In The Morning', 'Call Letter Blues', 'Idiot Wind' (all from the 16th); 'You're A Big Girl Now' and 'You're Gonna Make Me Lonesome When You Go' – in both slow and fast incarnations – from the 17th.

While they were cueing up these songs, Dylan was also listening for which songs could be further embellished. He had brought in the pedal steel player from New Riders of the Purple Sage, Buddy Cage, to see if he could enhance some tracks.

As Ellen recalls, 'The New Riders was one of the bands I repped as the head of A&R for the Columbia Records San Francisco office, and I loved Buddy's playing.' Such was her enthusiasm that when the New Riders had recorded 'You Angel You', from *Planet Waves*, she had proudly played it to her new boyfriend, who stored the information away for a rainy day, as was his wont.

That day came when he heard the sound of pedal steel rattling round his head for a few of the new songs. As a result, Cage was summoned to the third session, arriving at A & R around four o'clock on the 18th.

He would suggest to Sloman a few weeks later that he was afforded the chance to hear most of the new mixes: 'Bob played the tapes for me and said listen to them and play on whatever tracks you want. Frankly, there wasn't that much room on many of them for me … [But] the album's a beauty.' By the time Cage spoke to the ghost writer for Phil Ramone's 2007 memoir, his memory was no longer so reliable and the fish had become THIS BIG:

Buddy Cage: They played me a mess of tracks – maybe eighteen in all … The songs were so good the way they were that I wondered why they'd asked me to add anything to them. I looked at Dylan … 'I'd like you to put some steel guitar stuff over what's there,' he explained. 'Well, I honestly don't know where to begin,' I responded. Bob turned to Phil, 'Play them again.'

Though Ellen, like Tony Brown, can't quite remember if Cage played live on anything – he did not – she does distinctly 'remember others being in the studio for [the] various takes'. In fact, if Cage can be believed, Dylan was not only present, he was doing some coaching and/or cajoling during one song on which he was particularly keen for Cage to contribute:

Buddy Cage: I usually get the best hits in the first two or three times through … But [what I was playing on 'Meet Me In The Morning'] was not what Dylan wanted, apparently. He ended up flashing the light time after time after time, and I found myself having to do six or seven takes … I was getting really uncomfortable. Then finally the door to the control room opened, and Dylan came striding out, walks straight up to my steel, and sticks the toes of his cowboy boots under my pedal bar … and says, 'The first five verses is singin' – you don't play. [When] the last verse is playin' – you play!' … turns and strides back into the control room.

It doesn't sound like Dylan, and it isn't a story Cage shared at the time. His contemporary comments to Sloman do not contain the slightest hint of conflict. He is quite specific – and accurate – about what he worked on, 'I wound up cutting three tunes, two of which Bob kept.' Evidently, by mid-October he'd already been told – presumably by Ellen – that Dylan would be using his contributions to 'Meet Me In The Morning' and 'You're A Big Girl Now'.

The third song was evidently 'Call Letter Blues', which was also mixed on the 18th, when still in the frame for the album. If Cage's contribution to 'Call Letter' was not quite as stellar as on 'Meet Me In The Morning', both songs were never likely to appear on the same album, the former being little more than a musical facsimile of the latter.

According to the AFM logs, by eight o'clock Cage was done.[32] By then Dylan had begun to realise he might not yet be done with this album. He would have to tackle 'If You See Her, Say Hello', 'Buckets

[32] According to the AFM sheet, Cage contributed to something called 'Early In The Morning' – presumably a working title for 'Meet Me…' – plus 'Big Girl Now'.

Of Rain' and 'Tangled Up In Blue' afresh – and maybe 'Shelter From The Storm' (before he wisely changed his mind).

He elected to begin the reconfiguration with 'Buckets Of Rain', though his heart wasn't in it. The presence of a rival rock star wasn't helping. Mick Jagger knew all about the Dylan sessions because he was next door, mixing live tapes from the Stones' 1973 European tour for a King Biscuit Flower Hour radio broadcast, with Glenn Berger, during the day.[33] Indeed, according to Berger, 'We had to cram in the Dylan mixes after we were done.'

Actually, Berger simply surrendered his assistant engineer seat at the Dylan sessions to Rich Blakin, who would fulfill those duties for the remainder. And yet, the demoted engineer was apparently there for long enough to see the dynamic between this pair of rock heavyweights at work:

Glenn Berger: They'd apparently met before, but were not fast friends. These two titans in the rock pantheon couldn't have been more different. If Jagger was the most charming man on the planet, then Dylan … was the exact opposite. The two hung out together for a short while, but …[]… there was no rapport … Jagger, who was super-charming, thought Dylan was 'weird'. He was unfriendly to Mick at best. The whole thing was short and it fizzled.

Jagger had been angling for an invite since the previous evening, when Ramone can be heard at the end of a take asking if 'Mick' can come over about 10.30. When prompted, Dylan gives a slightly bemused 'okay'. (Steve Wilson, who had returned for a second helping on the 17th, confirms that Jagger did swing by at the end of this evening.) That evening could be the occasion when Berger felt a lack of rapport (or simply misread the signals). The A&R lady certainly remembers it differently:

Ellen Bernstein: There seemed to be an unspoken respect between Mick and Bob, especially since Mick seemed somewhat in awe of Bob and the songs … He was alone, as far as I can remember, and just completely stoked to be there.

[33] The first of the two Rolling Stones King Biscuit broadcasts would air on September 29th.

This makes a lot more sense, especially as Jagger would soon start to make his presence felt. Sloman's *Rolling Stone* report even describes the Stones singer as 'occasionally huddled with Dylan between takes'. Certainly by the 19th he was no longer such a wallflower, having assessed the lay of Dylanland.

On the 18th, as Dylan stumbles over the ending of an almost-realised first take of 'Buckets Of Rain', either Jagger or Ramone adopts a Bowery-bum voice to offer their solution, 'Get more wine.' Dylan has his doubts, 'I think I might have had too much. I'll try one more. If I don't get it…' He never finishes the thought, finally admitting, 'I just don't feel like it.'

Yet that first take starts so promisingly, his voice really warm, even if it hasn't yet got any *form*. It's presumably what Deliverance drummer Richard Crooks had in mind when describing 'one night [when] [Dylan] was in his cups – so bombed you'd think he wouldn't be able to play – but he was still going through the changes smoothly'.

Even so, Dylan's mind is soon wandering. Some mental block is stopping him from focusing on the task at hand, and there is an audible sigh from him when a second 'Buckets' stutters to a conclusion. Two more stabs at the song also break down. After both, Dylan asks Ramone to rewind the tape and erase the results. Thankfully, he doesn't,

Dylan soon admits to himself he 'just don't feel like it', and brings the session to a premature end. There is somewhere he would rather be, and that is at The Bottom Line, watching Little Feat. He leaves Jagger to his own bedspring symphony and Ramone to top'n'tail all those mixes, while he departs downtown with Ellen to see the Rock'n'Roll Doctor.

★★★

Fortunately, when Thursday evening comes around a revivified Dylan is determined to finish what he had begun on the Monday. Starting proceedings at seven, he has recalled Brown, and Brown alone, to (re)capture those last few tracks.

However, if Brown is thinking this will be like Tuesday – fourteen takes and home – he is soon disabused. It will be 3.30am before Dylan is satisfied. By then, he and Brown will have recorded no fewer than thirty-seven takes (six more than Monday's marathon), capturing eight songs whole.[34] It is, as Berger suggests, a case of Dylan 'record[ing] the album for a third time [in four days], this time just with the bass.'

Not that Berger is an eyewitness to the full proceedings, seemingly arriving when Jagger does. Blakin is now manning the desk, and seems to be under the illusion that Dylan cares what he thinks as they begin with 'Up To Me', Dylan hoping to put a little more of himself into some of the best lyrics he's written in years:

Rich Blakin: I was 27. Phil Ramone was the senior engineer on the project and Glenn Berger and I tag-teamed as assisting engineers. For reasons I will never know, I was assigned to be the lead engineer on one of the sessions … I saw Bob, about 25 feet away through the control room glass in the immense studio area … He warmed up a bit and when he was ready, I hit record, did the obligatory, 'We're rolling … take one,' and recorded the performance. … He looked toward the control room and said 'How was it?' [His] girl Friday … spoke, having good intentions, but I could see by Bob's facial expression that a candy-coated compliment was the last thing he wanted to hear … He looked at me and said 'How 'bout you?' … I reached out, held down the talkback switch, and said, 'Wanna check the guitar tuning and do another?'

If Blakin really did correct Dylan on his tuning, it was his first *faux pas* of the evening. Ramone can't have been pleased – or amused. He had gone out of his way to put Dylan at ease; to not let anything

[34] Fully half of the 'New York' *Blood On The Tracks* would come from tonight's taping.

get in the way when he was on a roll – and that included retuning his guitar:

Phil Ramone: You can't discard when you're working with Bob Dylan … You can hear noises on this record that you typically would have said, Let's do another take. His pick gets going on one or two songs, for example. I was able to reduce some of it, but that's almost part of the character, like the rattling mike stand. The next take, I would put a sandbag on the foot of the stand, but the take is there. There's no, 'C'mon Bob, we need another one.'

If Blakin really did breach the A & R code – and no such comment appears on either the multitrack or the two-track (which was once again running as a default record of proceedings) – he did not do it again. And though Dylan did not ask for his opinion again, he was certainly not about to stop consulting his Rosalind Russell.

In fact, the one time he is challenged on his guitar tuning, after a slow and bluesy acoustic 'Meet Me In The Morning', it is Ellen who calls him out, 'Hey Bob, I think you're a little out of tune.' He dutifully retunes his guitar and tries again.[35]

Actually, Ellen's voice provides regular reassurance at this final New York session. Having previously given only an occasional audible thumbs-up, she seems to sense a need for more encouragement tonight.

After dispatching an epic 'Up To Me' in a single take that bristles with a sorrow the first-night first take barely hinted at, Dylan elects to tackle 'Buckets Of Rain' – the song he struggled with the night before – only to stumble over the line, 'All you can do is do what you must'. But Ellen keeps her counsel, as she does through two more versions that fail to deliver the goods, timing her interventions.

Dylan is growing increasingly, audibly, frustrated. Before the second take he states, 'Let's just try and get it.' And after the third take stumbles, he is ready to call it quits, but knows he can't. To lighten the mood, he cracks a rare joke, 'This is hard, you gotta keep three or four things going at the same time. [Pause] Just like life!'

As he often does, he decides to switch songs and come back to it, informing Ellen and co. he's going to 'try 'n do "Up To Me" again'.

---

[35] Out of tune or not, this was the version released in 2012 on the b-side of 'Duqesne Whistle'.

But by the time Blakin has switched reels, he has changed his mind. He will persevere with 'Buckets Of Rain'. And, lo and behold, on the very next take those 'three or four things' come together 'at the same time'. At the end of the take, he suggests, 'That was my best shot.' This time Ellen is all reassurance, 'That was good.' Good enough to close the album in both incarnations.

With nary a pause, Dylan launches into a song he cut solo on night one and never looked back – 'If You See Her, Say Hello'. And just like tonight's 'Up To Me', he captures it in a single take. But still he looks for affirmation from behind the glass.

(This could be the moment Berger entered the studio to see how things were going, and heard what he thought was the line, 'It's a wonder we can even feed ourselves!' – but was actually, 'Tell her she can look me up if she's got the time'. If so, he misremembered what Dylan said, claiming he 'turned to the control room, and said, "Was that sincere enough?"' Actually, on this occasion, after the briefest of pauses, Dylan asks the muse behind the console, 'What d'ya think? Was it dramatic enough??' Ellen is quick to press playback, responding, 'It was real good.')

In just a matter of minutes, Dylan has taped two takes he thinks are good enough to be put on the album. Ellen enquires, 'D'you wanna hear that [back]?' But Dylan knows it is good and says, 'No, we're just gonna go on and do "Up To Me".'

This time he follows through and another 'Up To Me' sails past the seven-minute mark, prompting Dylan to ask if that was 'better'. Better than what? Presumably better than the equally great first take of the day. Ellen tries to encourage him: 'I thought it was great.'

Dylan seems a tad unconvinced. He asks, 'What was the matter with it?' to which Ellen guardedly responds, 'Nothing that I could hear.' At this point another voice – possibly Blakin's – steps in to suggest the guitarist 'hit some clinkers' – which might be the incident Blakin misremembered as involving 'guitar tuning'. Dylan, who is already steeling himself for another take, wonders aloud, 'I don't know if I got another one in me,' before finding the energy to throw himself into this vocal vortex again, producing the third complete 'Up To Me' of the evening. And it is another version he could have released. The pattern is set: Dylan switching between songs, never satisfied, always pressing on.

He clearly has a set of songs in mind to (re)record – most of the album, as it turns out – and won't allow himself to get stuck, having been in this same place and space at least once before: January 15th, 1965, Studio A.

On that occasion, eyewitness and lensman Daniel Kramer was visibly impressed by 'his method of working, the certainty of what he wanted, [as he] kept things moving. He would listen to the playbacks, discuss what was happening … and move on to the next number. If he tried something that didn't go well, he would put it off … In this way, he never got bogged down – he just kept going.'

That momentous day in '65 had resulted in seven songs (pruned from twenty mostly complete takes), with Dylan switching from full ensemble performances to playing solo or using twin acoustic guitars (with the late, great Bruce Langhorne). In the process, he captured definitive studio versions of 'Maggie's Farm', 'It's Alright, Ma', 'Gates Of Eden' and 'It's All Over Now, Baby Blue', all in *single* takes, while still finding the time to rock out on Maggie's farm and hit the road again. So he knew he could do it again, nine years on.

There was one song he kept returning to that January afternoon/evening; a song he should have had down. He had been playing 'Mr Tambourine Man' live since the previous May, recording it for his previous album with Ramblin' Jack Elliott.

But even that tongue-tripping lyric hadn't presented Dylan with as many problems as 'Up To Me'. This time, the words are not the stumbling block. It is the tone and tenor that is tripping him up. When he returned to it for a sixth take, he has already cut fourteen takes of five other songs, four of them destined for the fabled test pressing. And he still isn't satisfied.

At this point, the only song he has seemingly irrevocably abandoned is 'Meet Me In The Morning', which after two acoustic takes brings an audible sigh from Dylan and a barely audible, 'Well, whatever.'

When that moan fails to elicit a response from either Ramone or Ellen, he enquires, 'Was it any good? No? Was it *real* bad??' What it is, at this point, is simply a distraction. He is supposed to be reworking the likes of 'Tangled Up In Blue', and instead he is taking up tape with a song that's already been caught cooking.

Perhaps, as Dylan came around to the idea that the album should be essentially acoustic, he felt he needed an acoustic 'Meet Me In The

Morning' to make it *all* acoustic. Or perhaps he has just lost his way, as is indicated by another 'Buckets Of Rain', which he tries again after the second 'Meet Me In The Morning' and almost brings home.

But what he really needs is a 'Tangled Up In Blue' that satisfies his soul, because that moving-picture-in-song has always seemed like the jumping-off point for everything else.

When he finally turns his mind to this pressing matter, he runs down the opening verse twice[36] to ensure Brown is using the same imaginary chart, before starting in earnest. This time, when he does slip into the groove, he stays with it for the whole song. Even the clatter of buttons on his coat cannot distract him, though they have drawn their fair share of comment over the years. To Dylan, it matters not a jot:

Ellen Bernstein: There were certain ones where you can hear the sound of his fingernails on the guitar. That didn't matter to him. None of that stuff was important to him. What was important was the overall emotional weight of the song.

Perhaps he was even having a little joke at the complainers' expense when he made the 'clattering' version of 'Tangled Up In Blue' *the one*. The last sound listeners had heard on his previous album was the clatter of buttons on an acoustic 'Wedding Song'. Well, the first sound one hears on the New York *Blood On The Tracks* is those same damn buttons; perhaps his way of saying, *This is where we came in*.

If so, it's a gag lost on Phil Ramone, who continues to keep his thoughts to himself, reluctant to say, Let's do another take; suspecting any comment on his part will only make Dylan want to amplify the clatter. The one person who might persuade him otherwise not only understands Dylan's aesthetic, she embraces it:

Ellen Bernstein: He always seemed to want the mix[es] to be as authentic (and – my word – 'raw') as they could be – that's why there's the notorious sound of his fingernails on the guitar, which he really liked. So did I. I still do.

---

[36] The second breakdown seems to have been captured only on the two-track.

Having captured a 'Tangled' he was content to release, Dylan decided to (re)tackle the song which began life as its Siamese twin, 'Simple Twist Of Fate'. Here was another song on a shortlist of tunes he should have known he was not going to top. The exquisite second solo take from night one, mixed on the 18th, could hardly be bettered. Yet Dylan thought he might surpass it – or just wanted to see what it sounded like with the bass.

After chasing his own tail through one breakdown and two complete takes, he picked the second, a version listeners have lived with for years, and which personally I have always considered as close to perfection as folk-rock gets.

The very fact Dylan wanted to retackle both 'If You See Her, Say Hello' and 'Simple Twist Of Fate', and was even about to attempt 'You're A Big Girl Now', was a worrying sign. Key songs were starting to get away from him. And these were the very songs with which he had started proceedings three nights (aka a lifetime) ago.

Those versions of 'Simple Twist' and 'Big Girl' had already harnessed an intensity almost never captured once, let alone twice, such moments being as transitory as the wind. By now, though, Dylan had convinced himself he could improve on almost anything if he just stuck at it.

Over the next hour he would insist on tackling the two most ambitious lyrics he'd written for the collection, even though he had good mixes of both songs from that first dark night of the soul.

'Up To Me' was another song that clearly bothered him greatly. He was about to rack up three more takes (bringing the evening's total to eight) before capturing the fourth complete version of the session. And after all that effort, it would still fail to make the cut.

Was it too long at seven minutes and/or musically too similar to 'Shelter From The Storm'? Or just one epic too many? Ellen has a more prosaic explanation: 'I don't think either of us thought "Up to Me" was strong enough to include.' None of which serves to explain the tenacity with which Dylan pursued this elusive (and allusive) song, chasing it down at three separate points during that final session, yet catching it best (i.e. in its rawest state) on the first full take of the evening.

This eighth take is the one every fan knows from *Biograph* (1985). It is also the most musical, as Dylan finally figures out how to start the song on the beat, no intro, just straight into that remarkable opening line, 'Everything went from bad to worse, money never changed a thing.' But the vocal is mannered, and the way he (over) attacks the words tends to highlight incongruities (f'rinstance, I never really dug the way he sings 'real i-den-tit-y'), at the expense of a cohesive whole.

Nonetheless, in isolation it still puts the collected works of Neil Young into a cocked hat. Maybe he was just working himself into the state of mind he needed to tackle the one howling behemoth that still eluded him.

Like 'Up To Me', 'Idiot Wind' had taken an awful lot out of him on that first night. What he came up with in the end was a slightly detached vocal, only minutes after singing straight from a broken heart on the maddeningly incomplete take three.

Having decided to go with the complete take six of 'Idiot Wind', pulling it to master and doing a mix, rather than an edit of take three and take six as he at one point considered, he knew he could do better. He thus now girded his loins one more time, knowing this would be ten minutes of his life in the studio he would never get back.

Again, a little tutoring of Brown precedes the first serious take, which breaks down three minutes in. At least he seems to like what they have got going, and by take four he is again skirting the precipice, managing to stay out of the ditch for the full nine and a half minutes it takes to distill the pain of marriage down to one broken hallelujah. All sense of detachment has vanished and he is alone with himself. It is magnificent, with a capital M, and should have been released years ago.

But by now he has been living the songs for months and recording them for days (to Dylan's mind, the more daunting task), and he is no longer sure. As the hundred-second harmonica coda subsides into silence, a blown-away Berger recalls the moment: 'No one speaks … We [just] sat and waited. Just the sound of the tape machine still whirring: flap, flap, flap. Now the needle's still. … We waited [some more]. [Finally,] Dylan turned to the control room.'

What Dylan wanted to know was not, as Berger suggests, whether the take was 'sincere enough', but rather, 'Did they like it?' The 'they' includes not only Ellen, but also a curious Mick Jagger. Even after

Ramone, still a little stunned, assures Dylan 'they liked it', the *auteur* can't help but find fault with it, 'We fucked up a lot.'

This time the reassurance comes not from Ellen, but from Jagger, who takes it upon himself to offer some practical advice: 'There was only one place where it really fucked up. That was the first part of the harmonica bit at the end. Just cut that bit out.' He proceeds to ask Dylan if he wants to do it again – as if Dylan had it in him to climb that summit again. A drained Dylan simply asks, 'Can I listen to it?' He is done.

He has somehow pulled it off. He has his 'Idiot Wind' and a 'Tangled Up In Blue' he can live with, for now; a 'Buckets Of Rain' he can see closing the album; as well as versions of 'If You See Her, Say Hello', 'Simple Twist Of Fate' and 'Up To Me' that could all fit on an album he has spent six months conceptualising, standing on ever-shifting sands waiting for his ship to come in.

But he just can't let go. Not just yet. Surely, he tells himself, when I'm on a roll, it is my duty to keep rolling tape. What now ensues is a series of misguided attempts to (re)capture two songs he was never likely to supercede: 'Meet Me In The Morning', which he still wants to capture acoustic, and 'You're A Big Girl Now' – another song he has already got alive 'n' kickin' but is now thinking, maybe not.

The session has passed its meridian. Dylan is, by his own well-established criteria, 'wasting tape'. And yet, when he begins the long intro to 'You're A Big Girl Now', it seems as if he is once again stumbling towards an oasis of sound, only to find it is a mirage as he forgets the lyric after 'singing through these tears', a surefire sign he has gone beyond the song.

He now asks those on the other side of the glass, 'Is this paying off at all? Or [can you tell me] what's happening?' All that Ramone has to offer is, 'It's pretty, man.' This is not a Paul Simon session, though, and this man does not do merely pretty, or pleasant, or well-crafted. Dylan's a-propos-of-nothing response is to joke, off-mike, 'Nothing hurts, if you [don't] let it.'

Still digging that hole, he informs the engineers and his muse, 'Let's do "Meet Me In The Morning" and come back to this one.' He is running out of reasons to keep on keepin' on, but feels that he should. If the 'Meet Me In The Morning' turns out to be a bad idea, its harmonica coda is an even worse one.

Dylan wisely cuts it short with, 'I don't think we're gonna use that. Just file it! Stick it away.' But he won't give up. Off-mike, he is telling himself, 'If I could just do it softer.' As he begins a slightly different arrangement, Jagger makes another suggestion. It leads to a hilarious exchange which only proves that a man gotta know his own limitations:

Mick Jagger: Slide! Bob, you wanna play slide?
Bob Dylan: Who can play slide?
MJ: You.
BD: No, I don't wanna play slide.
MJ: You can play slide. Don't think it doesn't sound good, 'cause it does. [Dylan proceeds to play some slide – really badly.]
BD: Not me.
MJ: Okay, I agree. [Dylan laughs.]

If, in singing the blues, everything has gone from good to bad to worse, 'You're A Big Girl Now' – to which Dylan has now returned – has become a bird without wings. Try as he might, he can't get her airborne after two earnest attempts. Deep down, he knows the reason why: 'I can't get into it. We must have had it on that other one … We ain't gonna do it better. I just keep hearing that organ.'

But no sooner has he dispensed with 'Big Girl' than he starts toying with the idea of yet another 'Tangled Up In Blue'. Is he never gonna let it be? Already in the can are usable versions recorded with two guitars and bass on night one; bass and organ, *and* then bass and guitar on night two; and finally bass, guitar and buttons on night four. And yet he can't help himself. He continues to test the waters, even at half-two in the morning, perhaps hoping to cap off the session in style. Even after a couple of instrumental rehearsals and a false start, he perseveres.

Sure enough, he is soon off again in search of the same elusive *femme fatale*, Brown bringing up the rear. Well, strike me dumb, it turns out there really is another layer Dylan had not previously found, a way of bending the words that would not render them out of shape as well as a harmonica coda with all that 'tonal breath control' the others occasionally wandered from. The whole thing just takes one's breath away.

Even without the percussive clatter of fingernails and/or buttons, it is a performance which could (and perhaps should) have sat alongside the five performances from this night that do make it to the A & R acetates and CBS test pressing. But Dylan – and Ellen – end up preferring its clattering cousin.

No matter. It is a glorious end to four historic sessions. Ramone sums it up at take's end, asking the singer to 'imagine there was applause'. The last thing we hear on tape is the clunk of a guitar, followed by – one likes to imagine – Bob, Ellen and Mick waving goodbye to the A & R crew.

Jagger has his hour-long radio broadcast from the 1973 European tour which will constitute one of the classic Rolling Stones bootlegs, *Bedspring Symphony*, and Dylan has an album which he intends to let CBS release, but which will end up sharing the same pirate's cove as Jagger's; filling the coffers of The Amazing Kornyfone Record Label (TAKRL). For now, none of this matters. It is three in the morning and a huge weight has been lifted from Dylan's shoulders:

Ellen Bernstein: After the [final] session, Mick came with us to Shel Silverstein's apartment in the Village where we were staying, and we stayed up most of the night talking, and – I *think* – drinking Kahlúa and cream – ugh! ... I ran into Mick years later and he remembered me as being the girl in the control room with a giant stopwatch around her neck, which is vaguely accurate since I was keeping track of how long each song was.

(iv)

Blood On The Tracks *was another one of those records we went in and did in three or four days.*

—Bob Dylan to Cameron Crowe, Summer 1985.

Blood On The Tracks *did consciously what I used to do unconsciously. I didn't perform it well – I didn't have the power to perform it well – but I did write the songs. … The idea was right.*

—Bob Dylan to Matt Damsker, September 1978.

One can't help wondering if the topic of *Exile On Main Street* came up over Kahlúa and cream at Uncle Shelby's downtown shack, just before the dawn. A double album that would grow in critical stature year on year, it had been widely panned on its release for – among other crimes – being little more than an hour long, the Stones having wisely decided it needed all the sonic muscle they could spare. As such, they had spread its louche largesse over four capacious sides.

By the time Dylan and the girl with the giant stopwatch joined Ramone and Blakin at A & R the following Monday to approve final mixes, 'Call Letter Blues' was already out of the frame. Yet sacrificing 'Call Letter Blues' still left the pair caught between releasing an extravagantly long single album and an ultra short double. The eleven songs which Ramone remixed on the Monday (possibly bleeding into Tuesday), under Dylan's careful supervision, came to an eye-watering 61.30, making it only five minutes shy of *Exile On Main Street.*[37] The takes now pulled to master reels and (re) mixed were as follows:

16/9 Up To Me – Tk 1 solo [6.17]
16/9 Lily, Rosemary And The Jack Of Hearts – Tk 2 solo [9.50]
16/9 Meet Me In The Morning – Tk 1 with band [5.25]

---

[37] Berger has claimed that 'Dylan didn't show up for the mix … [He] didn't care about the recording thing. He left it in Ramone's hands.' Ellen is adamant, 'Bob and I were there for the mixing.' It would certainly be out of keeping for Dylan to absent himself at such a crucial stage.

16/9 Idiot Wind – Tk 6 with bass [9.01]
17/9 You're A Big Girl Now – Tk 2 with bass organ steel [4.23]
17/9 You're Gonna Make Me Lonesome – Tk 2 with bass [3.34]
17/9 Shelter From The Storm – Tk 4 with bass [4.56]
19/9 Buckets Of Rain – Tk 4 with bass [3.36]
19/9 If You See Her, Say Hello – Tk 1 with bass [3.25]
19/9 Tangled Up In Blue – Tk 1 with bass [6.51]
19/9 Idiot Wind – Tk 4 with bass [8.57]
19/9 Up To Me – Tk 2 with bass [6.23]
19/9 Simple Twist Of Fate – Tk 3 with bass [4.20]

The pair still intended to make *Blood On The Tracks* a single album. It meant at least one song would have to go and a couple of the others would need some pruning. They needed to lose at least ten minutes. The CD era was a decade away, and Dylan knew twelve-inch 33⅓ rpm vinyl signals begin to degrade above eighteen minutes per side. Any album over fifty minutes ran the danger of sounding thinner than wild mercury.

Yet at this stage there were still two takes of 'Up To Me' under consideration, and that song aside, there were three longer works, none of which Dylan was about to cut: 'Tangled Up In Blue', 'Idiot Wind' and 'Lily, Rosemary And The Jack Of Hearts'.

The mixes did not present a problem because as Berger notes, '[They] were just Dylan and the bass mostly, so the sound of the voice and the guitar was the whole thing.' Nonetheless, Berger recalls, 'Ramone spent a long time messing with the reverb – this was the signature Phil Ramone sound; he had these big boxes, called EMTs, in the basement that, when tweaked just right, made this beautiful echo, rich and evocative.'

Fortunately for fans of the understated, he had to deal at every turn with Dylan's determination to leave the sound 'raw'. There would be no sweetening, à la Paul Simon, to smooth out the rough edges.

By the end of the Monday, there were mixes of all thirteen takes, six of which had also been subjected to 'master' mixes on the 18th: 'Up To Me', 'Lily, Rosemary And The Jack Of Hearts', 'Meet Me In The Morning', 'Idiot Wind', 'You're A Big Girl Now' and (the fast) 'You're Gonna Make Me Lonesome When You Go'. Now Ellen and Dylan reluctantly accepted that 'Up To Me' would have to go:

Ellen Bernstein: I do remember that we played around with different sequences and then listened to them to see how they felt … I don't think either of us thought "Up To Me" was strong enough to include, and in fact I was later able to provide it to Roger McGuinn, another one of my artists [for *Cardiff Rose*].

Once 'Call Letter Blues', the slow 'You're Gonna Make Me Lonesome' and the exquisite solo 'Simple Twist Of Fate' – all mixed on the 18th – had also gone the way of all flesh, there was very little fat left to trim.

None, in fact. Fading down a rather nice harmonica coda on 'You're Gonna Make Me Lonesome' took away forty seconds, while clipping a whole verse from 'Meet Me In The Morning' – 'The birds are flying low, babe/ Honey, I feel so exposed' – removed a whole sixty-six seconds. But Lord Thomas and Ellen were clutching at straws.

Resolving the impasse would take time. Indeed, it would make the sequencing of *Blood On The Tracks* more laborious than the mixing. It would be over a fortnight before a final sequence was approved – after CBS had already logged the songs under a different sequence.

A week later on the 30th, one of the 'Up To Me' remixes was pulled to a 'master outtakes' reel along with a dub of the clattering version of 'Tangled Up In Blue' from the 19th, which still required Ramone to punch in the line, 'She was workin' in a topless place' (replacing the one originally sung, 'She was workin' in a roadside place').[38] At this juncture, acetates were made, one of which was forwarded to CBS in order to assign Job numbers for each track.[39]

The album was still coming in at 53.32, an unearthly length which put the long in long-player. However, there would be no more trimming, even if the sequence was still up for grabs. Indeed, the second side at this stage ran thus:

---

[38] So much for Ramone's claim that 'we only punched in things like a bass part or an organ note that went sour. Not on him. Definitely not on him!' The lines, 'You didn't trust me for a minute, babe/ I've never know the spring to turn so quickly into autumn' on 'Idiot Wind', also appear to have been punched in from another take at some point.

[39] Though Ellen has mislaid her acetate of Side A from the 30th, the Job numbers for the five songs on Side B correspond to her copy of the one-sided acetate she retained, not the final sequence.

1. Meet Me In The Morning   [CO 118940]
2. Shelter From The Storm   [CO 118941]
3. If You See Her, Say Hello   [CO 118942]
4. Jack Of Hearts   [CO 118943]
5. Buckets Of Rain   [CO 118944]

Actually, this sequence plays surprisingly well, putting the second side's nine-minute-plus epic in the same place as 'Idiot Wind' on side one. Yet the tinkering continued. By October 8th the ever-contrary Dylan, having settled on the familiar album sequence for side two, changed his mind about side one, which fleetingly ran as follows:

1. Tangled Up In Blue   [CO 118935]
2. Lonesome   [CO 118939]
3. Simple Twist Of Fate   [CO 118936]
4. You're A Big Girl Now [CO 118937]
5. Idiot Wind   [CO 118938]

By now, something else had changed. 'Idiot Wind' had acquired an organ overdub, which Ellen thought was 'a freaking great idea'. She may even have supervised the recording of it given that – according to the AFM log – Paul Griffin was hauled down to A & R at 10am, an hour when Dylan would certainly not have been up and about, to make another telling contribution to the album. The track sheets suggest he had at least four goes at it, before he came up with something spooky enough to put the wind up anyone.[40]

The October 8th acetate – evidently cut later the same day – contained the new mix on 'Idiot Wind' and a vocal punch-in on 'Tangled Up In Blue', but was otherwise essentially the mixdowns from the 23rd – minus both 'Up To Me's and the other 'Idiot Wind'. All that was needed now was for Dylan to revert to the original Side A sequence, and it would be time for a listening party; at which perhaps only Dylan would be really listening:

Rich Blakin: After all of the recording and mixing was done, CBS arranged for an intimate gathering, as dictated by the size of

---

[40] The four different organ overdubs may also mean that on the 2018 *Bootleg Series*, the preferred organ overdub/s may not correspond to the one on the test pressing as the quarter-inch of that mixdown appears to have been lost.

the control room. An elegant spread of wine, champagne, and hors d'oeuvres had been ordered for the occasion. Of the twenty-five or so people there, I knew, or knew of, around seven. Phil, Glenn and me. Then, of course, Bob. Seeming out of place to me at first sat a Hollywood actress and a Pulitzer Prize-winning writer. She was the same Shirley MacLaine you see on screen. No pretense. Legs crossed, cigarette held high. We made eye contact. Famous for his political satire, Art Buchwald leaned back deeply into the sofa, holding court, while fixated on the smoke rising from his giant cigar. Oh yes, one more. I was at the front office for a moment when I turned towards an opening elevator door. Mick Jagger stepped out – walked right up to me – held the sides of my head in his hands – kissed me square on the lips and said, 'Got any cocaine, mate?' Quite the entrance. I'm stationed behind the console, there to play the album back from a set of stereo safety master tapes, at a moderate level, through the control room speakers. There was music, conversation, and milling around. Suddenly, Bob seemed to be meandering his way, drink in hand, shades on, toward me. He stopped four inches from my face. He was about eye high. 'What did you do different?' he said … This was the last thing in the world I would have expected to be asked … See, I had mixed a few of the songs, Phil had mixed the rest … I said the first thing that came to mind, 'More reverb.' There was a pause, followed by the head gesture for okay, and he drifted away back into the crowd.

Rich Blakin

★★★

By now, the rumour mill was working flat out, and a number of people excluded from the listening party (but usually in the know) were anxious to hear the results. One of these was freelance journalist Larry Sloman, who found himself 'one day ... at Columbia records, hanging around, [when] I spied a sheet on the wall that documented the Dylan sessions. Of course, I jumped on that and proposed a piece in *Rolling Stone*, previewing the album. They agreed.'

Despite missing the boat, Sloman was prepared to swim around and see what he could find. Fortunately, it suited everyone involved – even Dylan – that the story now start to come out and the hype begin to build:

Larry Sloman: The sessions were already done by the time that I found out about them [but] once I got the info from Columbia, I started calling the Musicians Union and got in contact with the players. They all seemed happy to talk. I talked to Pete Hamill, through mutual friends, and he told me about the songs. This was before I heard the test pressing. I asked Pete to put me in touch with Bob, who was back in California. Bob called me at the *Rolling Stone* offices late one afternoon and we had a brief chat, and he confirmed some details of the sessions but he was at a phone booth and it wasn't enough time to get into anything substantive.

The piece, which ran in the November 21st, 1974, issue of *Rolling Stone* – under the headline, 'Dylan Looks Back' – hit the stands in early November. Already, some people were more enthused than they had been in a while about any Dylan album, starting with those directly involved with it.

Barry Kornfeld told Sloman, 'This is his first definitive LP in a long time, it's a return to 1965,' suggesting he must have heard more than just the last three songs on the 16th; while writer Pete Hamill, whom Dylan had specifically requested write the liner notes, was almost lost for words:

What I love about Dylan is what he leaves out, because then he gives us a chance to help create it ... Dylan leaves the spaces ... I can't really find the language to describe these songs. The album is just fucking wonderful.

The reaction everywhere was overwhelmingly positive, starting with Sloman himself, who was afforded the chance to hear one of the earliest test pressings by someone at Columbia. He was 'also able to hear it repeatedly from a friend of Bob's, who had a copy'. His reaction was typical, 'I thought the NYC sessions were so much more intimate, more cutting to the bone [than what came out] … so much more emotional and chilling.'

Those test pressings were doing Dylan's (and CBS's) work, as they were meant to. By November one of them had made its way into the hands of the West Coast promotion man, a major Dylan fan and important cheerleader:

Paul Rappaport: I played it to friends in the company, I played it for the [people in] radio, because I thought it was one of the greatest things ever, and when he decided to change it, me and a handful of others at Columbia were heartbroken. Because we thought we had heard one of the most perfect recordings of all time. You didn't [usually] share test pressings … with many people … [But] I would sit with people and I would get a bottle of wine and I'd say, You're gonna sit here with [a] glass of wine and you're going to listen from beginning to end, and you're not going to utter a word. And every person I played it for was just so moved [by] the end, they couldn't talk.

Even the decision to put the release of the album back to New Year's Day (from the original November 1st, 1974, never a very practical plan) was working in the album's favour, even if it had been the result of a last-minute switch of sequence and Dylan's decision to change the cover from 'a shot of a huge red rose on a white background' to a more conventional portrait in profile – the second time in two albums Dylan induced a delay in release-date by changing the cover at the death.[41] This time, thankfully, there was no promotional tour to latch onto, nor any interviews the emotionally naked savant was planning to give.

[41] According to Sloman's *Rolling Stone* story, 'Dylan was [also] reportedly hunting for old photos of himself performing at Gerde's Folk City for the back sleeve.'

But all the while Dylan was alone in LA, internal doubts were daily growing. Reflecting on his recording career to date, in the notebook where first he sketched out rough ideas for 'Tangled Up In Blue' and 'Idiot Wind', he now caustically observed it had 'only served to take me across the desert. Okay, now let's get back to life.'

To assuage his concerns, he first visited the two Robs, Robertson and Fraboni, co-producers on his previous LP, *Planet Waves*, who were busy building their own studio, Shangri-La.

Robbie Robertson: He [said he] had done some recording in New York. I was curious to hear what he'd cut, and he played me an early version of *Blood On The Tracks*. It was tough, bold and dark, more powerfully personal than anything I'd heard him do in a long time.

If Robertson is foggy on the details, erroneously believing that Dylan's childhood friend Louie Kemp was there, his 2016 memoir entirely removes Rob Fraboni or that Dylan specifically asked Robertson to ask him 'to come over there, so he could play [us both] the record'.

Like Sloman, Fraboni was someone who wanted to relive the experience, 'So I asked Robbie, do you have any blank cassettes? Bob didn't know I recorded it ... We both said, It's great, we love it ... Bob wanted our opinion.'

Dylan continued seeking reassurance. According to Glenn Berger, he even took to occasionally calling Phil Ramone mid-session: 'We'd be in the control room recording, and the phone would ring ... I'd hear Phil say, "Bob, it's amazing. Really. Probably your best album ever. Don't worry. It's great." Phil and I would look at each other and shake our heads in disbelief. Dylan, insecure? Huh? This went on week after week, increasing in intensity as we approached the New Year deadline.'

When George Harrison, the one Beatle to have become a close friend of Bob's, was passing through LA on his ill-fated Dark Horse tour, he was also privy to a private listening session, the experience staying with him through what was a dispiriting return to touring. He was unable to share these feelings with anyone until he arrived in New York in early December, where a trepidatious *Rolling Stone* reporter assigned to interview him ventured backstage:

Larry Sloman: By the time [the tour] came to New York there was already a scathing article in *Rolling Stone* putting down the show because Harrison wasn't playing the old hits. So when I show up from *Rolling Stone* I was persona non grata. But Bill Graham ... arranged an interview with George for me when the tour hit the Garden. I was led into Harrison's dressing room in the bowels of Madison Square Garden ... To break the ice, knowing he was a huge fan of Bob's, I asked him straight off whether he had heard the acetate of Bob's new album. He immediately lightened up. 'How great is "Tangled Up In Blue"?' ... and we both started to sing the song.

And still Dylan wasn't sure the songs displayed both reason and rhyme. Nor by this time was he gauging his feelings with that previously reliable barometer, Ellen. She 'had absolutely no idea that he had any intention of re-recording any of the tracks. I thought it was as close to a perfect musical creation as had ever been recorded. Frankly, I was devastated when he rerecorded songs ... He did it without consulting me [which], of course, was his right as the artist and creator.'

How late Dylan made his decision to rerecord half the album we can only guess, but it was presumably after December 16th, when CBS filed the track details into their cardex system,[42] and it seems a close relative played a part. According to a January 1975 entry in *Rolling Stone*'s 'Random Notes': 'His September sessions in the Big Apple [had] made the news ... but the tracks didn't sit well with Bob. He headed north-west, where brother, Dave Zimmerman ... lent a hand with the album's corrective surgery.'

The suspicion has always been that David did more than 'lend a hand'; he stuck his oar in, voicing his concern that the album was not musical enough. Guitarist at Sound 80 studios, Kevin Odegard, who knew Zimmerman Jnr. well, recalls being told by David of him informing Dylan, 'You know this isn't going to be a radio record unless you do something to it,' after the elder brother asked him what he thought.

However, on the one occasion Dylan himself was asked about his motivation by Cameron Crowe in 1985, he suggested he simply

[42] Intriguingly, said cardex also suggests the tapes were now in San Francisco, which did have a CBS mastering facility at the time.

decided to change horses in midstream: 'I had the acetate. I hadn't listened to it for a couple of months ... The record still hadn't come out, and I put it on. I thought the songs could have sounded different, better, so I went in and rerecorded them.'

This was certainly the story the godfather of rock criticism, Paul Williams, heard on the grapevine in the seventies: 'The album was ready to go, maybe even being pressed, and – as I heard the story – Dylan listened to his copy while visiting Minneapolis near Christmastime and decided to try again. He went into a studio there with some musicians his brother turned him onto.'[43]

The one time Dylan was called out on his decision by one of the few contemporaries whose name could be mentioned in the same sweet easy breath, he was rather evasive about his reasoning. As Joni Mitchell later told a credulous David Yaffe:

> One night I had a party here ... and Bob crashed it. And the bootleg of the first *Blood On The Tracks* was playing ... And I said, 'Why didn't you put that out?' And he said, 'Somebody stole the tape.' ... The Minnesota sessions were not touching at all. He asserted himself again as a man ... He went and recut it with his brother in Minnesota. They butchered it ... Originally, the writing ... was more vulnerable, and the orchestration was subtle, very like when I was using just a little of that stuff to [embellish] my performances ... It was beautiful.

One person who was not about to confront him about his choices – even on those occasions when their paths crossed again, as they did through 1978 – was fair Ellen, who was still in the employ of CBS. She was firmly in the Joni camp, even if she certainly would never have portrayed Dylan's revisionism as a case of 'assert[ing] himself again as a man':

Ellen Bernstein: There was no way I was going to be happy with the new tracks, and I wasn't. I was profoundly disappointed but in the end I understood that perhaps on some level he had become uncomfortable with the level of vulnerability he had expressed in

---

[43] Williams was in a consensus of one when he went on to write, in 1980, 'Those [Minneapolis] recordings are among Dylan's finest; the earlier versions are not just inferior in most cases, but actually bad,' an extraordinarily wide-of-the-mark remark by one of rock's more astute critics.

the original recordings. I respected that, even though I felt like something unique had been lost.

At least Ellen experienced that disappointment in real time. She was one of the 'fortunate' few who were sent an acetate of the finished album with the five Minneapolis substitutions, three of which acted as the set's supporting pillars, 'Tangled Up In Blue', 'Idiot Wind' and 'Lily, Rosemary And The Jack Of Hearts'. And yet by January 1975, *Rolling Stone* was already reporting that 'Dylan's mid-30s romantic lurchings seem to have ended. Months ago, rumors blew … of an imminent marriage break-up, but Bob is back with Sarah and the kids.'

A possibility remains that Dylan originally intended merely to tinker with the New York album, not gut it. We have contemporary firsthand testimony that he might have been looking to change just one or two songs and got a bit carried away (as he would again in 1992, when he reversed the process by going into his garage studio to record 'a couple of songs' to fill out an all-electric album of folk covers he'd made that summer in Chicago, only to end up with the all-acoustic *Good As I Been To You*).

When local musician Chris Weber arrived at the first of the Sound 80 sessions on December 27th, bringing with him the Martin acoustic guitar he was looking to sell, he informed *Insider* magazine the following month:

> Bob seemed to be preoccupied with what was going to take place, the recutting of some of his songs for his Columbia album, *Blood On The Tracks*. He was very friendly, though, relaxed and laid back … I found out that he wasn't too happy with the original recording of the album, and wanted to have different takes of his tunes, so that he could decide which cuts he liked the best.

But, as anyone who ever worked with the man knows, he almost always prefers the latest version, rarely allowing himself the luxury of A-B'ing the earlier version/s of a song before going with his gut.[44]

What Dylan certainly didn't allow himself through the holidays of '74 was the same luxury he had enjoyed in the weeks after the A & R sessions,

---

[44] It is a trait Neil Young has also been guilty of, with equally hit-and-miss outcomes.

living with these performances and playing them to people he trusted. By the time he turned up at Shangri-La Studios in the new year with this recast version of his masterpiece, the 'unmaking' was a *fait accompli*:

Rob Fraboni: In January he shows up at Shangri-La with a dozen copies of the album. Bob puts on 'Tangled Up In Blue'. Robbie and I look at each other, [as if] to say, 'What the hell happened?' We loved that other record. Robbie said [after Bob left], 'Leave it to Bob. He makes these kinds of choices.'

Robertson later remarked, 'This new version was more uptempo and energetic, but the first recordings he played for me still stuck in my mind,' reflecting the near-universal response of those lucky folk able to have made the comparison in real time; one of whom had been doing his job, playing his test pressing to anyone who was prepared to sit still for an hour and just listen:

Paul Rappaport: I had two thoughts [when I heard the released album: one,] this isn't anywhere near as personal, meaningful or powerful as the other one. [Two,] the other one might have been too personal for Bob, so he hid behind a more rock version [on] certain songs. 'Cause when you listen to the original, it is one long love letter: I love you – I hate you – why can't we be smarter than this? – you're an idiot – I'm an idiot – all the things you would tell a woman, but written by a genius ... As a promotions person, I tried to have an open mind and say [to myself], 'Well, some of these new versions are good. They're not bad [anyway]. It's still an amazing record.' [But] it's just not what it was.

Perhaps the most dismayed individual confronted with the Minneapolis tracks after living with the memory of those A & R performances – used and unused – for months, was the poor assistant engineer who was assigned the task – a matter of some urgency – of splicing the old and new versions together into one master.[45] It needed to be forwarded to a panicking record label posthaste. They were

---

[45] This was done in double-quick time. The quarter-inch stereo master is dated January 3rd, just four days after the second Sound 80 session. In their haste, they sped up – as per Dylan's instructions – (most of) the album but left the last three tracks uncorrected. (See Appendix IV.)

already sitting on a quarter of a million printed sleeves (and had yet to realise that the liner notes on the back cover related to an album which was no longer the one they planned to insert in those inner sleeves):

Glenn Berger: When we returned from the holiday, Phil sat down with me, pale and dispirited. Bob had panicked. He was visiting his family in Bemidji, Minnesota, and over the Christmas break decided to rerecord the album ... The only studio and musicians available were from Sound 80, the local jingle studio, where they recorded commercials for Mom's Biscuits and the local Oldsmobile dealership. It was my job to cut out the tracks we worked on, and splice in the new ones recorded there. As I did so, I listened to the new recordings. Dink, doink, dink doink, bum, bum, bum, "We're idiots babe, it's a wonder we can even feed ourselves . . ." This searing, wrenching, burning, bloody song turned into a happy little jingle!

The released 'Idiot Wind' – with an overdubbed vocal that went against Dylan's whole cut-it-live ethos – was also the one song which served to annoy Tony Brown, who 'really thought that what Paul Griffin and I did was far superior to what was used on the final album. Nothing can touch our version of "Idiot Wind".' Hard to argue with that assessment. Nor did Brown have to rely solely on his memory, despite Dylan failing to include him on the list of lucky recipients for a test pressing because he had 'a friend at Columbia who gave me an acetate [sic] of the New York album':

Tony Brown: In my opinion, the New York versions of 'Idiot Wind' and 'Big Girl Now' were stronger. [But] I didn't have a problem with the other Minneapolis tracks; their 'Tangled Up [In Blue]' was clearly better.

In fact, 'Idiot Wind' became the veritable eye of a particular storm when the album was released, as elements of the US music press planted the idea – inspired by the very nature of the Minneapolis version of that song, it would seem – that Dylan's primary emotion when writing and recording these songs was rage.

As such, when *Rolling Stone* ran a symposium on the album in its March 13th, 1975 issue – after giving the record the magazine's usual lukewarm review of Dylan product – several of its better-known contributors seemed obsessed with the idea that the album was a series of rain unravelled rants:

> By reaffirming our avatar's capacity for rage, *Blood On The Tracks* clarifies not only his artistic continuity but also the limits of his vision, devoid as it is of broad generosity. – **Robert Christgau.**

> Dylan, when he's angry, cannot be matched, not by anyone. He's got his critical vision back and … realizes at long last that this is the seventies, and it pisses him off. – **Chet Flippo.**

> Like no other singer/poet, Dylan at his best transmutes personal frustration, anger, self-pity and moral intolerance into an inspired litany of rage and remorse. – **Stephen Holden.**

It was an accusation that would be levelled at this record long after it had departed from the charts; one which Lester Bangs, back to his belligerent best, used to beat Bob up metaphorically, when he made an entirely different record seven months later.

By Bangs's own admission, he had begun by 'initially dismissing [the 1975 album] on one hearing as a sprawling, absurdly pretentious mess whose key was the ridiculously spiteful "Idiot Wind",' only to find himself 'drawn back to it repeatedly by a current that I was not at all convinced was entirely wholesome'. Bangs's own abusive lifestyle and cycle of arch-cynicism, driving even those who loved him away, were now apparently failings he could lay at Dylan's door. Yet by the time Bangs was firing his pistol-whipped prose at this sitting duck, plentiful evidence of the unbelievable truth had entered the public domain.

The inevitable had happened – and with remarkable alacrity, even by most bootleg brigands' standards. A bootleg LP of the New York alternates had appeared in select outlets across the nation.

As has been documented, a surprisingly large number of people on the outer layers of the onion had been able to hear – and/or own – a copy of the fabled CBS test pressing. Paul Rappaport – 'Rap' to his many friends – was one lucky possessor of such a pressing. He was also smart enough to realise, 'You had to be very careful. Of course

I didn't leave it with anybody. [But] in those days test pressings were sent to a fair number of people. So if I'm the regional [promotions] guy in LA … how many regional people would have got it?'

It was Rap, though, who was the man with a copy in LA, the nation's hotbed of bootleggers. A fair few music-minded folk took note. Unfortunately, playing the album on so many occasions was itself a risk. Sure enough, on one such occasion, Rap remembers, 'I bumped the turntable once – [so] there's a scrunch [on 'Idiot Wind'].'

That 'scrunch' would duly be immortalised when some sneaky Pete – without Rap's knowledge – managed to covertly dub his pressing and pass it to Dub Taylor's ex-partner, Ken Douglas, at TAKRL, now TMQ's main rival label in LA's bootleg emporium.

Once TAKRL realised that what they had was a version of the album which Dylan had scrapped, there could only ever be one outcome – a bootleg facsimile of the missing (half-) album, called *Joaquin Antique*, linked intuitively to some of the songs on *Bringing It All Back Home* he had previously reworked electrically.

Dylan himself could have precious few complaints. Given the widespread pirating – as he would have seen it – of the original *Freewheelin'* and the so-called 'basement tape' 14-song acetate (which between them gave birth to the whole era of bootleg-album-as-commercial-product phenomenon), he surely would have known the New York album would probably come back to haunt him.

Pulling an album from the schedule barely a fortnight before it goes to the pressing plant, when you are the most bootlegged artist in Christendom, is not merely asking for trouble, it is inviting it in for a three-course meal and a bottle of wine.

Dylan was predictably put out. The cat was out of the bag, and boy, was he pissed. Even when that original, fast-tracked bootleg version of *Blood…* was hastily recalled – ironically, because the skip on 'Idiot Wind' coincided with a pressing fault – it was followed by the free circulation of the New York test pressing on cassette (this being the era when cassette bootlegs started to be traded widely without money trading hands, just for the love of music).

As inevitable as death and taxes, further bootleg vinyl versions followed, in the guise of *Passed Over & Rolling Thunder* – one of the great Dylan bootleg albums, featuring both the electric set from

Newport '65 and a cleaned-up version of the New York *Blood On The Tracks* tracks – and its single disc cousin, *Blood Takes.*

If Dylan had copped out by re-recording the songs in a way which made him seem less vulnerable, it had all been in vain. And if he now sat in a painter's studio in the south of France quietly fuming, there were at least two people intimately involved with the making of said masterpiece who felt a certain vindication:

Phil Ramone: [The New York] *Blood On The Tracks* was an outpouring of the man's life, in a very troubled time for him, and this was almost cathartic for him in the studio. It was incredible.

Ellen Bernstein: I was so happy when the original versions became available and everyone could experience what I experienced from the first day he felt comfortable enough to trust me with witnessing the creation of what I still believe was one of the epic creations of his legendary career.

For Ramone, the stain remained. Though he had merely 'engineered' those magical sessions, it was at his studio and had *his* sound. Not surprisingly, he came to feel that what should have been his peak achievement had been taken away from him.

As a final irony, Ramone would end up spending a fair amount of time with Kevin Odegard, the guitarist who brokered the sessions at Sound 80 which changed the whole nature of the released record. Odegard, ever the diplomat, usually steered clear of a topic that continued to irk the iconic producer:

Kevin Odegard: Phil and I rubbed shoulders often in the eighties and early nineties, not always happily. Rarely, if ever, did we discuss *Blood On The Tracks* directly. When it did come up, I was careful to focus on his brilliant career and redirect the discussion away from [the album] as soon as possible. It was always a sore spot for Phil. I knew that his blood pressure would spike if it came up, and he'd clam up around me to avoid bashing me outright for participating in the despoiling of his Dylan legacy. *Blood On The Tracks* was a project about which he was rightfully proud and righteously pissed off for the rest of his life.

For Ellen, the memories remain warmer and fonder, bound up as they inevitably are with a relationship which spawned the one set of post-accident songs which to this day resolutely escapes the long shadow cast by Dylan's pre-accident achievements. For her, this album will always be so much more than a musical momento of a summer romance:

Ellen Bernstein: I've never forgotten the feelings of being a part of [it] all …. even though it was a really really long time ago … I was twenty-four and had loved music since I was fourteen. And I loved Bob, as much as I could at that age and at the level of truth and naiveté that defined my limited experience of the world as a girl from San Francisco via Ashtabula, Ohio.

For Dylan, too, the feelings remain, forever preserved in plastic. For that is the nature of the recording artist; his (or her) work trapped not in amber, but in vinyl. Even though he pulled the plug on the New York *Blood On The Tracks* – ensuring that said album failed to reach the shops – it remains the benchmark for all confessional albums. One of these days, surely, it shall be released.

Albums/Dylan, Chi-Lites, Lennon, Wailers.

SIGNS OF LIFE

A great month for albums, with Dylan's latest offering heading the list.
Michael Gray thinks it's rather good.

Bob Dylan

Blood On The Tracks
CBS 69097

I don't know how, but some adjustment in our consciousness must now follow from the fact that it is Bob Dylan who has produced, in *Blood On The Tracks* the most strikingly intelligent album of the seventies.

That seems to me to change everything. It transforms our perception of Dylan—no longer the major artist of the sixties whose decline from the end of that decade froze seminal work like *Blonde On Blonde* into a historic religious object which one chose either to put away in the attic or to revere perhaps at the expense of today's music. Instead, Dylan has legitimised his claim to a creative prowess as vital now as then—a power not, after all, bounded by the one decade he so much affected, but capable of being directed at us effectively for perhaps the next thirty years.

Changed too must be our blueprint of how rock music moves forward. This has been that artists come and go in relatively short time-spans, with new people emerging to make the major changes. Careers are presumed to peak early and then slide into inevitable decline.

Blood On The Tracks demolishes that pattern.

It addresses the seventies and our darkness within, with a whole arsenal of weapons—albeit weapons from Dylan's past. It has as much sheer freshness as his or anyone else's first-ever album; as much genuine urge to communicate; as much zest. Yet it combines them all with a sharp wit and intelligence, and an impeccable judgement, so that the sum of these parts is a greater whole than either the Dylan of the sixties or any artist since ever brought to rock.

The album deals, among much else, with the overlaying of the past upon the present, the inexorable disintegration of relationships, and the dignity of keeping on trying to reintegrate them against all odds.

Gone, utterly, is Dylan's recent myopic, wilful insistence on eternal love, on its wholesome cocoon; in its place is a profoundly-felt understanding of our fragile impermanence of control.

'Tangled Up In Blue' deals with the way in which many forces—past upon present, public upon privacy, distance upon friendship, disintegration upon love—are further tangled and repossessed by time. It's a scintillating account of a career and a love affair, and how they intertwine. It becomes a viable summary of the last fifteen years through one man's eyes, and in its realism and mental alertness it offers those of us who believe that (in Dave Laing's phrase) one sugar-shortage does not an apocalypse make, a vigorous alternative to all the poses of wasted decay that most 'intelligent' rock has been marketing in the seventies. (In 'Shelter From The Storm' Dylan takes a direct swipe at these apocalypse-freaks, in this barbed and mocking aside: "Do I understand your question, man, is it hopeless and forlorn?!")

'Idiot Wind' covers similar territory. It is less consistently successful than 'Tangled Up In Blue' but far more ambitious, and where it does work fully, it yields truly visionary poetry—the strongest imagery and the greatest sense of life experienced on a razor's edge that Dylan has ever achieved.

Seen first as a sort of 'Positively 4th Street Revisited', it isn't very successful. The too-personal bone-scraping of 'Someone's got it in for me/They're planting stories in the press . . . /I haven't known peace and quiet for so long/I can't remember what it's like . . . /You'll find out when you reach the top/You're on the bottom . . . "—that jars. It also produces, in Dylan, a need to step back from that personal quality somehow: and he does it the wrong way, by stylising the anger so that some of his delivery has the same *faked* passion that spoilt *Before The Flood*.

Yet this is a small element in the song. It deepens into one of infinitely greater emotional range than 'Positively 4th Street'. The idiot wind that blows is the whole conglomerate of things which assail our integrity; and the song locks us in a fight to the death, in a contemporary graveyard landscape of skulls and dust and changing seasons. Destruction and survival again.

The preoccupation with this just-possible survival one must fight for is evoked in its most urgently eloquent in this unsurpassable stanza:

"There's a lone soldier on the cross/Smoke pourin' out of a box-car door/You didn't know it, you didn't think it could be done:/In the final end he won the war/After losing/Every battle . . .?"

That is matched, later in the song, by the extraordinary tugging wildness of this—a triumph of poetic strength: "The priest wore black on the seventh day/And sat stone-faced while the building burned/I waited for you on the runnin' boards/Near the cypress tree while the springtime turned/Slowly to autumn/Idiot wind/Blowin' like a circle around my skull/From the Grand Coulee Dam to the Capitol . . . " (And what a rhyme!)

The 'you' is an every-changing element in the song. It certainly isn't a simple object/victim at which Dylan is directing his venom. In an almost explicit demonstration of this near end of the song, he deals with his love affair one more time, and starts with a truly universal cameo of how it feels to live with someone when the wall has gone up between them.

"I can't feel you anymore/I can't even touch the books you've read/Every time I crawl past your door/I can't wishin' I bin somebody else instead."

That isn't venom or dismissal or blame. From there, Dylan deepens it further with another devastating burst of poetry: "Down the highway/Down the tracks/Down the road to ecstasy/I followed you beneath the stars/Hounded by your memory, an' all your/Ragin' glory . . . /I kissed goodbye to the howling beast/On the borderline which separated you from me . . ."

Astounding stuff.

With *Blood On The Tracks*, without question, Dylan has decimated utterly the idiot winds of "Dylan's a fat millionaire gig" and "Dylan's gone soft in the head". This album is the work of a man who has never been of sharper intelligence nor more genuinely preoccupied with the inner struggles and complexities of human nature. His sensibility is 100% intact.

Appendix I
They're Planting Reviews In The Press

If proof were needed that the release of Blood On The Tracks *was a landmark event, the fact that just about every heavyweight from the golden age of rock criticism weighed in with their opinions – some of them hilariously wide of the mark (Davey, babe) – rather confirms it. Here is a smattering of some of the wiser, and wilder, contemporary remarks from this legion of rock proselytizers…*

In his liner notes to the new Bob Dylan album, *Blood On The Tracks* (CBS), Pete Hamill, who not so long ago was writing his very human articles for the *New York Post*, says: 'here is Dylan, bringing feeling back home. In this album he is as personal and as universal as Yeats or Blake; speaking for himself, risking the dangerous opening of the veins, he speaks for us all.'

Hamill writes well. He's a Dylan fan. So am I. There are lots of us still left. And with each album Dylan has released in the past few years we've been hoping it's as great as *Blonde On Blonde* or *John Wesley Harding* or *The Times They Are A-Changing*.

Maybe, when sufficient time has elapsed to provide a proper historical perspective, it will be possible to mention *Planet Waves* in the same breath, but for me, and most of those fans I would think, that feeling hasn't quite been there.

And that, in a deep sense, is because it's not really true, as Hamill says, that in speaking for himself Dylan 'speaks for us all'. Dylan long since ceased to do that, except in the most clichéd sense…

The man's hold on his generation has slackened off, I would suggest, and this was one of his strengths. After all, a fundamental rule of pop success is to seize the time. Dylan is an artist, above and beyond chart positions, and yet his self-involvement now, a powerful source of his fascination, is not as frequently absorbing as it was.

I wonder that he bothers to say, in 'Idiot Wind' – probably the strongest song on this album, however – that 'someone's got it in for me/they're planting stories in the press'. For him it's such an empty gesture. His ability these days to express broad truths out of highly personal emotions is less in evidence than it was.

Michael Watts, *Melody Maker* 25/1/75.

To all the musical back-ups 'sparse' is something of an understatement; 'stark' would be a little more accurate – but that's not even the point. The melodies are fascinating simply because they're almost non-existent.

Dylan himself seems to be admitting this in his utilization of the blues form on two tracks: 'Meet Me In The Morning' and 'Buckets Of Rain'. And when he does attempt a melody, it never fails to carry distinct echoes of past efforts.

The first track, 'Tangled Up In Blue', crackles with the same chord progressions and 'feel' as the *Before The Flood* retread of 'Lay Lady Lay'; 'Simple Twist Of Fate' utilizes the same stanza framework as 'I Want You' crossed with the descending chord-pattern that George Harrison used for 'Something'; and 'Idiot Wind' rings out structured like 'One Of Us Must Know' echoed through 'Like A Rolling Stone'.

And here again, it's not simply that Dylan has lost his melodic inventiveness. From his performances on this album Dylan seems to have become almost tone deaf.

In fact, not only are his vocals the worst he has ever allowed to be etched in vinyl, his guitar playing is often out-of-tune, and the accompaniments often so trashy they sound like mere practice takes (the organ on 'Idiot Wind', for example, could only have been vamped spontaneously on a single play-back).

Okay, okay – so now you're thinking I'm building up to some horrendous put-down of the whole product. Which couldn't be further from the truth really. Already I'm enthralled with this album to a point where I can't even remember a time before where I've been *this* drawn to a recorded work.

It's not that it's *good* Dylan. In fact, I don't honestly know what *good* Dylan *is* anymore. The Bob Dylan of *Blood On The Tracks* is a changed man – wasted (his melodic and vocal sterility bears that out), fatalistic, and fairly desperate from what I can see…

In 1965, Bob Dylan wrote 'I accept chaos. I am not sure whether it accepts me.' Back then it was just a pretty cool thing to say – the Dada King throwing a random gem of wisdom to all the hep-cats who could dig where Bobby was coming from. Now he's learning just what it was he said. The hard way.

Blood On The Tracks is deeply flawed, almost pathetic. For, here we are face-to-face with a man who has played one too many games with his image and his audience – the ultimate distant persona brought to his knees.

I recall, when *Planet Waves* was about to be released, thinking that the only way Dylan 'the artist' could pull himself together with any semblance of integrity would be to strip himself bare and make a statement as chillingly personal as Marlon Brando did through *Last Tango In Paris*.

In *Blood On The Tracks*, I feel he has achieved precisely that – and, to that extent, all the bullshit about 'Dylan is back' and 'his best since *Blonde On Blonde*' is utterly superfluous.

Blood On The Tracks, despite its manifold flaws, makes statements that overshadow anything currently being put out in the rot of the medium to a point at which comparisons cease to exist.

Nick Kent, *NME* 25/1/75.

When he reappeared [after the motorcycle accident] he seemed to be living a life which came awfully easy. *Nashville Skyline* said he was completely content. To find Dylan in the midst of an enforced calm (some called it flaccidity) came as a blow to anyone who took the caged thrashings of *Blonde On Blonde* seriously. *Nashville Skyline* and *Self Portrait* talked about everything but Dylan, and *New Morning*, while heartening in places, was still a little hard to take. Hard to believe that life could be that easy.

Which has to account to some large extent for the popularity – and aesthetic appeal – of *Blood On The Tracks*. Pain is universal, pleasure is not. Dylan, miraculously, is again remembering the things we forgot to say. He may never have wanted to, but he has caught in tone and substance the process of aging, of living.

Blood On The Tracks strikes me as *Another Side Of Bob Dylan* ten years on ... with one critical difference ... *Blood On The Tracks* deals exquisitely with self-consciousness. Dylan no longer has the option simply to live; he is always BOB DYLAN ... Therefore his sources of experience are tainted, and his songs must either reveal that or deal with it directly. *Blood On The Tracks* does a little of both. It is an extraordinary album. The question isn't whether it is Dylan's best album since *Blonde On Blonde*, but whether it is *the* best album since *Blonde On Blonde* ...

It had to have been hard to write, perform and release *Blood On The Tracks*. But where perhaps in recent years he would have hidden or withheld his nameless revelations, Dylan has propelled himself onto centerstage with them. Perhaps because he wanted to, perhaps because he had to.

Peter Knobler, *Crawdaddy* [4/]75.

I don't know how, but some adjustment in our consciousness must now follow from the fact that it is Bob Dylan who has produced, in *Blood On The Tracks,* the most strikingly intelligent album of the seventies.

That seems to me to change everything. It transforms our perception of Dylan – no longer the major artist of the sixties whose decline from the end of that decade froze seminal work like *Blonde On Blonde* into a historic religious object which one chose either to put away in the attic or to revere perhaps at the expense of today's music. Instead, Dylan has legitimised his claim to a creative prowess as vital now as then – a power not, after all, bounded by the one decade he so much affected, but capable of being directed at us effectively for perhaps the next thirty years.

Changed too must be our blueprint of how rock music moves forward. This has been that artists come and go in relatively short time-spans, with new people emerging to make the major changes. Careers are presumed to peak early and then slide into inevitable decline.

Blood On The Tracks demolishes that pattern.

It addresses the seventies and our darkness within, with a whole arsenal of weapons – albeit weapons from Dylan's past. It has as much sheer freshness as his or anyone else's first-ever album; as much genuine urge to communicate; as much zest. Yet it combines them all with a sharp wit and intelligence, and an impeccable judgement, so that the sum of these parts is a greater whole than either the Dylan of the sixties or any artist since ever brought to rock.

Michael Gray, *Let It Rock* April 1975.

What is Dylan saying about his relation to the past? ... I hear simple major-key melodies, a Dave Van Ronk guitar, inimitable harmonica and organ passages, Biblical images, blasts of anger, flashes of humour, on-the-road restlessness. One side of the record is dominated by a tale of romance, robbery and murder called 'Lily, Rosemary And The Jack Of Hearts', its lyrics belong on *John Wesley Harding*, its sound on *Highway 61 Revisited*. The other side has 'Idiot Wind', which sounds – at first – like a classic Dylan hate song ... Yet it's clear that this album is not just a seductive throwback. A new kind of naked grief ... haunts the quiet, ethereal beauty of songs like 'If You See Her, Say Hello' and 'Simple Twist Of Fate' ... Dylan sings in half a dozen different voices, all of them familiar but not quite placeable ...

You could say that *Blood On The Tracks* is about Bob Dylan's estrangement – physical or spiritual, literal or symbolic, permanent or temporary – from a woman, or from woman. I would say that it's pretty obviously about his own marital troubles ... [But] the facts aren't really important, what matters is that on this record the relationship between Dylan's self and his persona seems richer, scarier and more intense than it has in years.

Ellen Willis, *The New Yorker* 7/4/75.

He has saved phrases from our culture's rhetorical slagheaps and centered them so singularly that they lease new life. He shoots juice to banality simply by kicking everything up several notches – best seen in the way these aren't love songs, not love songs alone, but songs to his *audience* as lover. That's no new trick for Dylan – he was performing it as early as 'It's All Over Now, Baby Blue' ... But he hasn't so consciously built an album around it before this one, which begins and ends talking to the audience as lovers.

William Lhamon Jnr., *The New Republic* 5/4/75.

I have already played this record more times in the past week than I play most records in a year. I love it. It is one of Dylan's best albums. It is probably the best album of the last five years. No matter how broke and busy you are, you can't go wrong by going out and purchasing this record right now. End of review ...

Blood On The Tracks is so fucking beautiful. Just to focus in on one aspect, where is there anyone around today who can sing half this well? I wanted to slug someone at a party recently who was repeating that old canard about Dylan being good in spite of his singing. People don't know what singing is. It's delivery. So-and-so may have a pair of vocal chords that should be put under glass and

kept in the Smithsonian; what I want to know is, how much do I
hear when that voice speaks to me? Is there an audible, complex
consciousness present in the enunciation of every noun, verb and
pronoun? When there is, it's not because of the words. Any fool
can think, and most can write; *delivering* those thoughts intact to
another mind, another consciousness, is the extraordinary talent.
Every singer currently working the rock circuit would be well-
advised to shut up for a year and just listen to and consider Dylan's
diction on this album.

Paul Williams, *Soho News* 30/1/75.

Bob Dylan wasn't kidding when he called this album *Blood On The
Tracks*; the songs are covered with it. It's an album of wounds – just as
casual listening fills one with delight at Dylan's testing of his genius,
a close listening can be shattering, terrifying. It goes without saying
that no one else in rock & roll could make a record like this.

Greil Marcus, *Rolling Stone* 13/3/75.

If this is some sort of breakthrough, that's only because it's more lucid.
The theme – the (failure of) salvation through women – is identical
with (but reversed [from]) *Planet Waves* … And though the music
and lyrics may echo his greatest work, that's all they do. The long
songs, particularly, suffer from flat, tangled imagery, and the music,
with all its hints at the old glory, is often incompetently performed.
I suppose it's all a matter of what you're willing to settle for.

Dave Marsh, *Rolling Stone* 13/3/75.

Although *Blood On The Tracks* is aptly named and surely shoulders
a fair share of pain, it is hardly the bleak, desolate wasteland of
pessimism and self-hatred which critics have claimed. Far from it.
Dylan's subtlety, intelligence, depth of feeling and overall artistry
have created a flexible and complex ambiguousness which somehow
fuses an elegiac tone with the most muscular, confident style …
Even the near anonymous, ordinary Minneapolis musicians do
better than the more gifted but overrated Band … This album is
vital and alive, its despair tempered throughout with the joy of
being a survivor.

Paul Nelson, *Rolling Stone* 13/3/75.

When *Blood On The Tracks* was released, I felt as ambivalent about it as I was about its subject matter and I remained that way. After initially dismissing it on one hearing as a sprawling, pretentious mess ... I would get drunk and throw it on, finding profound aphorisms alternating with oblique poetry, belching outbursts of muddled enthusiasm ... Then I would sober up and it would sound, once again, dull, overlong, energyless, the aphorisms trite and obvious, the poetry a garbled parody of the old Dylan. But I persisted; there was *something* there that mattered to me and I ultimately found out what it was. I discovered that I only really wanted to play this record whenever I had a fight with someone I was falling in love with ... At length, I concluded that any record whose principle utility lay in such an emotional twilight zone was at worst an instrument of self-abuse, at best innocuous as a crying towel and certainly was not going to make me a better person or teach me anything about women, myself or anything else but how painfully confused Bob Dylan seemed to be.

Lester Bangs, *Creem* **April 1976.**

322 WEST 48th STREET
NEW YORK, N.Y. 10036

Womack Org

Dolored

CLIENT: CBS
ARTIST: Dylan   PROD: _____
DATE 9-19-74 STUDIO: 1   W.O. # ____ ENG. P.L.
☐ 4 TRK   ☐ 8 TRK   ☒ 16 TRK   ☐ ASSOC. ENG
☒ ORIG.   ☐ SAFETY
NOTES: _____

TANGLED UP IN BLUE (REVISED) TAKE No: DATE: 9-19-74
BOB AGT BoB AGT BDBS BoBS
SAFETY SONY 421 1187 SAFETY

TLE SIMPLE TWIST OF (REVISED) TAKE No: DATE: 9-19-74
BoB AGT BoB AGT BDBS
Safety Sony 421 U-87 Safety

TLE UP TO YOU (REVISED) TAKE No: 2-RL5 DATE: 9-19-74
BoB AGT BoB AGT BDBS
Safety Sony 421 U-87 Safety

IDIOT WIND (REVISE) TAKE No: DATE:
ORG H1 BoB AGT BoB AGT BDBS BDBS ORGAN LOAN ORGAN H1N ORGAN LO H1 ORGAN MSTR
5/3 9/3 Safety Sony 421 U-87 Safety 5/5 5/5 8/3 8/3 5/4

A & R RECORDING, INC.
322 WEST 48th STREET
NEW YORK, N.Y. 10036
JU 2-1070

STEREO MIX
DOLBY

1 OF

Date 9-23-74 Studio A Client CBS Artist DYLAN WO # Eng HC
☐ Mono ☐ Two TRK. ☐ 4 TRK. ☐ 8 TRK. ☐ 16 TRK. ☐ Orig. ☐ Safety ☐ Copy Producer:

TAKE	TITLE	TIME	COMMENTS	TAKE	TITLE	TIME	COMMEN
1	TANGLED UP IN BLUE OUTTAKE	RL4					
2	TANGLED UP IN BLUE COMPLETE	RL4	start	NG			
3	BIG GIRL NOW	RL2					
4	SEE HER SAY HELLO	RL4					
5	SHELTER FROM STORM	RL3					
6	BUCKETS OF RAIN	RL4					

ORIGINAL

Appendix II
**A New York *Blood On The Tracks*
Sessionography, 16-23 Sept, 1974.**

PTM = Pulled to Master.
NIK = Not in Krogsgaard sessionography.
Mono only = Only on mono reference tape.
BOTT = Blood On The Tracks *LP.*
TP = Blood On The Tracks *test pressing.*
INC = Incomplete Take
FS = False Start

Where 'revised' appears in this sessionography, this is because the track has been duly noted this way on the session sheets. This usually means that the take numbers begin again, from one.

September 16th, 1974
All tracks exist on mono and rough multitrack reels, except where noted.
01 If You See Her, Say Hello Tk 1 solo.
02 If You See Her, Say Hello Tk 2 solo. PTM. *Bootleg Series 1-3.*
03 You're A Big Girl Now Tk 1 solo.
04 You're A Big Girl Now Tk 2 solo. PTM.
05 Simple Twist Of Fate Tk 1 solo.
06 Simple Twist Of Fate Tk 2 solo. PTM.
07 You're A Big Girl Now Tk 3 solo.
[Includes. 30-second snatch of 'Up To Me' at beginning.]
08 Up To Me Tk 1 solo. PTM.
09 Lily, Rosemary And The Jack Of Hearts Tk 1 solo. Mono only. NIK.
10 Lily, Rosemary And The Jack Of Hearts Tk 2 solo. PTM. TP.
11 Simple Twist Of Fate Tk 1A with band.
12 Simple Twist Of Fate Tk 2A INC with band.
13 Simple Twist Of Fate Tk 3A with band.
14 Call Letter Blues Tk 1 with band.
15 Meet Me In The Morning Tk 1 with band. BOTT [edit].
16 Call Letter Blues Tk 2 (or 3) with band. PTM. *Bootleg Series 1-3.*
17 Idiot Wind Tk 1 INC with bass. Mono only.
18 Idiot Wind Tk 2 INC with bass. Mono only.
19 Idiot Wind Tk 3 INC with bass.
20 Idiot Wind Tk 3A insert with bass.

21 Idiot Wind Tk 5 FS with bass. Mono only.

22 Idiot Wind Tk 6 with bass. PTM. *Bootleg Series 1-3.*

23 You're Gonna Make Me Lonesome Tk 1 INC with band.

24 You're Gonna Make Me Lonesome Tk 2 INC with band.

25 You're Gonna Make Me Lonesome Tk 3 INC with band.

26 You're Gonna Make Me Lonesome Tk 4 with band. Mono only.

27 You're Gonna Make Me Lonesome Tk 5 with band. Mono only.

28 You're Gonna Make Me Lonesome Tk 6 FS with band. Mono only.

29 You're Gonna Make Me Lonesome Tk 7 INC with band. Mono only.

30 You're Gonna Make Me Lonesome Tk 8 with band.

31 Tangled Up In Blue Tk 1 with bass and second guitar.

September 17th, 1974

All tracks exist on multitrack reels.

01 You're A Big Girl Now (revised) Tk 1 with bass and organ.

02 You're A Big Girl Now (revised) Tk 2 with bass and organ + pedal steel overdub. PTM. TP. *Biograph.*

03 Tangled Up In Blue (revised) Tk 1 with bass and organ.

04 Spanish Is The Loving Tongue Tk 1 INC. NIK.

[Includes brief blues jam at end of song.]

05 You're Gonna Make Me Lonesome (revised) Tk 1 with piano.

06 Shelter From The Storm Tk 1 with piano. *Jerry McGuire* s/t [no piano].

07 Buckets Of Rain Tk 1 with bass.

08 Tangled Up In Blue Tk 2 with bass. PTM. *Bootleg Series 1-3.*

09 Buckets Of Rain Tk 2 with bass. PTM.

10 Shelter From The Storm (revised) Tk 2 with bass.

11 Shelter From The Storm (revised) Tk 3 INC with bass.

12 Shelter From The Storm (revised) Tk 4 with bass. PTM. BOTT.

13 You're Gonna Make Me Lonesome (revised) Tk 1 with bass. PTM.

14 You're Gonna Make Me Lonesome Tk 2 with bass. PTM. BOTT.

September 18th, 1974

All tracks exist on rough multitrack reels.

01 Buckets Of Rain (revised) Tk 1 INC solo.

02 Buckets Of Rain (revised) Tk 2 solo.

03 Buckets Of Rain (revised) Tk 3 INC solo. NIK.

04 Buckets Of Rain (revised) Tk 4 INC solo. NIK.

September 19th, 1974

Tracks 1-30 exist on two-track and multitrack reels; tracks 31-37 multitrack only.

01 Up To Me (revised) Tk 1 INC with bass.

02 Up To Me (revised) Tk 2 with bass.

03 Buckets Of Rain (revised) Tk 1 with bass.

04 Buckets Of Rain (revised) Tk 2 INC with bass.

05 Buckets Of Rain (revised) Tk 3 INC with bass.

06 Buckets Of Rain (revised) Tk 4 with bass. BOTT.

07 If You See Her, Say Hello (revised) Tk 1 with bass. TP.

08 Up To Me (revised) Tk 1 INC with bass.

09 Up To Me (revised) Tk 2 with bass.

10 Up To Me (revised) Tk 3 with bass.

11 Buckets Of Rain fragment with bass. NIK.

12 Meet Me In The Morning (revised) Tk 1 with bass. 'Duqesne Whistle' 45.

13 Meet Me In The Morning (revised) Tk 2 with bass.

14 Buckets Of Rain (revised) Tk 30 per BD with bass.

15 Tangled Up In Blue (revised 2) rehearsal with bass.

[Two-track includes an additional false start.]

16 Tangled Up In Blue (revised 2) Tk 1 with bass. TP.

17 Simple Twist Of Fate (revised) Tk 1 INC with bass.

18 Simple Twist Of Fate (revised) Tk 2 with bass.

19 Simple Twist Of Fate (revised) Tk 3 with bass. BOTT.

20 Up To Me (revised) rehearsal with bass. NIK.

21 Up To Me (revised) Tk 1 INC with bass.

22 Up To Me (revised) Tk 2 with bass. *Biograph.*

23 Idiot Wind (revised) Tk 1 INC with bass.

24 Idiot Wind (revised) Tk 2 INC with bass.

25 Idiot Wind (revised) Tk 3 INC with bass.

26 Idiot Wind (revised) Tk 4 with bass. TP.

27 You're A Big Girl Now (revised) Tk 1 INC with bass. NIK.

28 You're A Big Girl Now (revised) Tk 2 INC with bass.

29 Meet Me In The Morning (revised) Tk 1 INC with bass.

30 Meet Me In The Morning (revised) Tk 2 INC.

31 Meet Me In The Morning (revised) Tk 3 INC with slide.

32 You're A Big Girl Now (revised) Tks 3-5 INC with bass. NIK.

33 You're A Big Girl Now (revised) Tk 6 INC with bass. NIK.

34 Tangled Up In Blue (revised 3) rehearsal with bass. NIK.

35 Tangled Up In Blue (revised 3) Tk 1 INC with bass.

36 Tangled Up In Blue (revised 3) Tk 2 INC with bass.
37 Tangled Up In Blue (revised 3) Tk 3 with bass.

Songs pulled to master at the end of September 17th session:
If You See Her, Say Hello
You're A Big Girl Now
Simple Twist Of Fate★
Up To Me★
Lily, Rosemary And The Jack Of Hearts★
Meet Me In The Morning★
Call Letter Blues★
Idiot Wind★ – all from 16/9
You're A Big Girl Now★
Buckets Of Rain
Shelter From The Storm
You're Gonna Make Me Lonesome When You Go [slow]★
You're Gonna Make Me Lonesome When You Go [fast]★
Tangled Up In Blue – all from 17/9

★ – asterisked songs remixed on the 18th from the master reels.

September 18th, 1974 [mixing session]
1974 0917 13 You're Gonna Make Me Lonesome (revised) Tk 1
[3.47] slow. Stereo remix.
1974 0917 14 You're Gonna Make Me Lonesome Tk 2 with bass.
[3.34] BOTT.
1974 0916 06 Simple Twist Of Fate Tk 2 solo.
[5.12] Stereo remix.
1974 0916 08 Up To Me Tk 1 solo.
[6.04] starts at 0.20. Stereo remix. Master Outtake reel.
1974 0916 10 Lily, Rosemary And The Jack Of Hearts Tk 2 solo.
[9.55] TP.
1974 0916 15 Meet Me In The Morning Tk 1 with band.
[5.25] BOTT [w/ overdub + one verse edited].
1974 0916 16 Call Letter Blues Take 2 (or 3) with band.
[4.33] *Bootleg Series 1-3.*
1974 0916 22 Idiot Wind Tk 6 with bass.
[9.03] *Bootleg Series 1-3.*

1974 0917 02 You're A Big Girl Now (revised) Tk 2 with bass and organ + pedal steel.
[4.33] TP/ *Biograph*.

September 23rd, 1974 [remix session]
1974 0916 08 Up To Me Tk 1 solo.
[6.04] starts at 0.20. Stereo remix. Master Outtake reel.
1974 0916 10 Lily, Rosemary And The Jack Of Hearts Tk 2 solo.
[9.55] TP.
1974 0916 15 Meet Me In The Morning Tk 1 with band.
[5.25] BOTT [w/ overdub + one verse edited].
1974 0916 22 Idiot Wind Tk 6 with bass.
[9.03] *Bootleg Series 1-3*.
1974 0917 02 You're A Big Girl Now (revised) Tk 2 with bass and organ + pedal steel.
[4.33] TP/ *Biograph*.
1974 0917 14 You're Gonna Make Me Lonesome Tk 2 with bass.
[3.34] BOTT.
1974 0917 12 Shelter From The Storm (revised) Tk 4 with bass.
[5.09] BOTT.
1974 0919 06 Buckets Of Rain (revised) Tk 4 with bass.
[3.36] BOTT.
1974 0919 07 If You See Her, Say Hello (revised) Tk 1 with bass.
[3.36] TP.
1974 0919 16 Tangled Up In Blue (revised 2) Tk 1 with bass.
[6.57] TP. Still clattering buttons.
1974 0919 26 Idiot Wind (revised) Tk 4 with bass (no organ overdub).
[9.31] TP [w/ overdub].
1974 0919 22 Up To Me (revised) Tk 2 with bass.
[6.43] *Biograph*.
1974 0919 19 Simple Twist Of Fate (revised) Tk 3 with bass.
[4.32] BOTT.

The Working Notebooks: A Brief Precis

Notebook #1: [October 1973 to October 1974]
Dylan Archive, Tulsa, OK.
p1 – 'too busy, too stoned' verse from Tangled Up In Blue.
p3 – verse; part Tangled/ part Simple Twist.
p6 – mentions [Idiot] Wind; Grand Coulee Dam to Omaha.
p17-18 – 'Montague Street' verse from Tangled Up In Blue; Idiot W. lines.

Notebook #2: [March to July 1974, all appear to be pre-Loretto]
Dylan Archive, Tulsa, OK.
p1 – proto-verse for Meet Me In The Morning + You're Gonna Make Me.
p2 – You're Gonna Make Me Lonesome draft.
pp3-4 – Idiot Wind 'buttons of our coats' verse.
p4 – You're Gonna Make Me Lonesome draft.
p4 – 'Little Tiger', unfinished song idea.
p5 – You're Gonna Make Me Lonesome (cont.)/ Up To Me – rhymes for 'ee'.
p5 – Idiot Wind (cont.)
p6 – 'Fishing On A Muddy Bank', unfinished song idea.
p7 – You're Gonna Make Me Lonesome (cont.)
p8 – Idiot Wind (cont.)
p9 – 'You Were Good To Me', unfinished song idea.
p11 – 'Blind Alley', unfinished song idea.
p14 – 'Blazing Star', unfinished song idea.
p15 – 'The Pouring Down Rain', unfinished song idea.
p16 – Idiot Wind (cont.)
pp17-18 – Idiot Wind (cont.)
p20 – 'Selfish Child', unfinished song idea.
p22 – 'Don't Want No Married Woman'.
p24 – 'Horse Thief', unfinished song idea.
pp25-29 – Tangled Up In Blue, multiple drafts.
pp30-33 – multiple fragments, inc. unfinished song idea: 'Atheist'.
p34 – Simple Twist Of Fate.
p35 – 'You're Too Big For Your Britches', unfinished song idea
p35 – 'White Song Ghetto Money', unfinished song idea + Big Girl Now.
pp36-37 – Simple Twist Of Fate (cont.)
p38 – 'Ain't It Funny'.

pp39-41 – Lily, Rosemary And The Jack Of Hearts.

p42 – Tangled Up In Blue (cont.)

p43 – Simple Twist Of Fate (cont.)

p44 – Idiot Wind (cont.)

p45 – 'Dusty _____ Blues' aka Tangled Up In Blue.

pp46-53 – Lily, Rosemary And The Jack Of Hearts (cont.), multiple drafts.

p54 – Unknown song idea about persecution of the Jews.

p55 – Lily, Rosemary And The Jack Of Hearts (cont.)

p56 – Unknown song idea, possibly early version of 'It's Breakin' Me Up'.

p58 – 'There Ain't Gonna Be Any Next Time'.

p59 – 'Belltower Blues'.

p60 – Unknown song idea, possibly called 'Iron Bell'.

p61 – Unknown song idea, possibly called 'Don't Want No Conversation'.

pp62-63 – Unknown song idea, possibly continuation of 'There Ain't Gonna Be Any Next Time'.

pp63-65 – Shelter From The Storm.

p66-67 – 'There Ain't Gonna Be Any Next Time' (cont.).

p68 – 'Blood On The Ice', unfinished song idea + 'There Ain't Gonna Be…'

p69 – Narrative story with reference to 'postal clerk' verse in Up To Me.

p70 – 'There Ain't Gonna Be Any Next Time' (cont.).

pp71-72 – 'Death Is Inside Me', unfinished song idea.

Notebook #3: ['Fair Copy', July/August 1974]

Morgan Library, NY.

pp1-5 – Lily, Rosemary And The Jack Of Hearts.

pp7-9 – Tangled Up In Blue.

p11 – You're A Big Girl Now.

p13 – 'There Ain't Gonna Be Any Next Time'.

pp15-17 – Shelter From The Storm.

p19 – 'Belltower Blues'.

pp21-22 – If You See Her, Say Hello.

p23 – 'Church Bell Blues' [aka Call Letter Blues].

p25 – 'Where Do You Turn?'

p27 – 'It's Breakin' Me Up'.

pp28-29 – Simple Twist Of Fate.

pp30-34 – Idiot Wind 1.

p35 – 'Don't Want No Married Woman'.

p37 – You're Gonna Make Me Lonesome When You Go.

pp38–40 – Idiot Wind (rewrite).

pp41–43 – Up To Me.

pp45–46 – Up To Me (rewrite).

p47 – 'Ain't It Funny'.

p49 – 'Little Bit Of Rain'.

pp51–52 – Idiot Wind (2nd rewrite).

pp52–53 – song fragments inc. one verse of Buckets Of Rain.

33 1/3 RPM   STEREO
10/8/74   S-19322

BOB DYLAN

                           SIDE A

1. TANGLED UP IN BLUE 6:48
2. LONESOME 3:53
3. SIMPLE TWIST OF FATE 4:18
4. YOU'RE A BIG GIRL NOW 4:22
5. IDIOT WIND 8:50

799 SEVENTH AVENUE
New York, N. Y. 10019

33 1/3 RPM   STEREO
10/8/74   S-19322

BOB DYLAN

SIDE B

1. MEET ME IN THE MORNING 4:24
2. LILLIE, ROSEMARY & THE JACK OF
           (9:50)   HEARTS
3. IF YOU SEE HER SAY HELLO 3:23
4. SHELTER FROM THE STORM 4:59
5. BUCKETS OF RAIN 3:21

799 SEVENTH AVENUE
New York, N. Y. 10019

COLUMBIA

Reference recording

Bob Dylan

33rpm   Stereo
Side 1   Ⓟ 1975 CBS Inc.

1. Tangled Up In Blue   5:40
2. Simple Twist of Fate   4:18
3. You're A Big Girl Now   4:36
4. Idiot Wind   7:45
5. You're Gonna Make Me
   Lonesome When You Go   2:58

TT: 25:23

COLUMBIA

Reference recording

Bob Dylan

33rpm   Stereo
Side 2   Ⓟ 1975 CBS Inc.

1. Meet Me In The Morning   4:19
2. Lily, Rosemary and the
   Jack of Hearts   8:50
3. If You See Her, Say Hello   4:46
4. Shelter From The Storm   4:59
5. Buckets of Rain   3:29

TT: 26:30

Appendix IV
Blood On The Tracks on Vinyl,
Official and Unofficial: A Jotted Down Note

In 2018, even with the release of six CDs' worth of *Blood On The Tracks* material, purchasing a true representation of what went down in New York in September and in Minneapolis in December 1974 on vinyl – the medium it deserves to be heard on – remains well nigh impossible.

Even the bootleggers seem to have dropped the ball. Though an excellent double-CD from the moribund bootlegger Scorpio (called simply *Blood On The Tracks Sessions*) put into the public domain an ultra-clean transfer of the New York test pressing and the five songs from Minneapolis at the correct speed – from the 1981 Columbia Mastersound half-speed master (see later) – a truly bloody awful 11-track bootleg CD, *Blood On The Tapes*, drawing on seven officially released tracks and an EQ'd copy of the test pressing, seems to be better known and more widely distributed. Avoid like the plague.

The murky history of the album on vinyl goes all the way back to September 25th, 1974, and what purports to be an A & R acetate of the final New York album. The two labels to this (presumably double-sided) acetate were first reproduced by Michael Krogsgaard in *Master of the Tracks* (SSRR, 1988), and on the face of it appeared to be genuine.

Only when pukka A & R acetates turned up from September 30th and October 8th, did doubts begin to be raised. For starters, the sequence on the 25th was exactly the same as the released album. And yet, neither of the later acetates follow the same order. We are thus required to believe that Dylan had the final sequence two days after mixing the album, only to spend two more weeks trying out different sequences (and not just trying them out – cutting them to acetate).

Other aspects of the labels also failed to ring true. The songs have no timings, there is no S-# for the acetate, and the date is above the record speed (33⅓ rpm), when these should have been reversed. Also, two of the songs are mistitled, in a way that corresponds to no known studio log, AFM sheet or acetate: 'Shelter From Your Storm' and 'Meeting In The Morning'. Don't sic twice, it's all right.

Finally, and most tellingly, if such an acetate was cut on the 25th, the 'Idiot Wind' (from the session on the 19th) would have been without the organ overdub, and no such recording has ever circulated. As it stands, I think a certain wariness as to their authenticity justifiable.

This being the case, the first known version of the album in 12" form is a one-sided acetate of a provisional side-two sequence dated five days later. This acetate is assigned the number S-19257. There was undoubtedly an S-19256, which had a sequence, possibly different, for side one, and that would also have an unoverdubbed 'Idiot Wind'. The sequence for side two ran as follows:

B1 Meet Me In The Morning 4:24
B2 Shelter From The Storm 4:59
B3 If You See Her, Say Hello 3:23
B4 Jack Of Hearts [sic] 9:50
B5 Buckets Of Rain 3:21

The next acetate to emerge from A & R [this one two-sided – S-19322] was made eight days later, only a few hours after Paul Griffin added his organ to 'Idiot Wind'. Save in sequence, this acetate is in every way identical to the Columbia test pressings from which all bootleg versions of the original album would spring. This time it was the first side which departed from the now-familiar sequence, thus:

A1 Tangled Up In Blue 6:48
A2 You're Gonna Make Me… 3:53
A3 Simple Twist Of Fate 4:18
A4 You're A Big Girl Now 4:22
A5 Idiot Wind 8:50

Within a matter of days, side one had been resequenced, and a limited number of Columbia reference pressings were being made, initially as acetates and then in the form of test pressings with the telltale Columbia Reference Recording black & white label. This was the album that Dylan played to Rob Fraboni, Robbie Robertson and George Harrison, and it ran thus:

A1 Tangled Up In Blue 6:48
A2 Simple Twist Of Fate 4:18
A3 You're A Big Girl Now 4:22
A4 Idiot Wind 8:50
A5 You're Gonna Make Me… 3:53 TT: 27:27

B1 Meet Me In The Morning 4:24
B2 Lily, Rosemary And The Jack... 9:50
B3 If You See Her, Say Hello 3:23
B4 Shelter From The Storm 4:59
B5 Buckets Of Rain 3:21 TT: 26:01

Engineer and archivist Joel Bernstein now takes up the story, having compared and contrasted every acetate and test pressing he could find:

> The tape playback speed of all tracks on all acetates up to this point are the same as the record speed of 15 ips, so that the pitch and tempo of all tracks is as performed. Having heard an acetate in which the five performances from Minnesota replaced five of the performances from the New York sessions, Bob then asked to have another acetate cut with the same edit and sequence, but with the tracks slightly sped up, as, according to Ellen, he was concerned that the 'tracks were dragging', i.e. the tempos were too slow. That sped-up version, in which most (but not all) of the tracks were intentionally sped up slightly (as best I can tell, 2%) during playback. That is apparently the version which Bob approved. All subsequent versions of the album, including the released vinyl LP and CD, were made. The only exception is the 1981 Columbia Half-Speed Mastered vinyl reissue, in which all tracks are presented at their native speed, pitch and tempo ...
>
> This is the version of the album that first had me thinking about tape playback speed. When I first played a copy, in 1981, it was apparent from listening to the first few tracks on each side that the tempos were slower and pitch was lower than the album as it had been released in 1975 ... Then in 1994, when Clinton Heylin was visiting while working on his *Bob Dylan Behind Closed Doors* book, I arranged for us to speak on the phone with Ellen Bernstein. Among the many interesting parts of her account of being with Bob during the writing and recording of the album, was that at some point Bob was worried that the song tempos were dragging, and that he'd asked to have an acetate made with the songs slightly sped up to increase the tempos overall.

Unfortunately, whoever carried out Dylan's instructions clearly 'bodged' the job, as the first seven tracks on the released album have indeed been sped up, but the last three have not. So the released album is neither fish nor fowl. Nor is it very likely Dylan wanted it done this way as the last three tracks are not all from New York or Minneapolis, but rather one is from Minneapolis, two are from New York, making it another fine mess from the great Columbia label. The quarter-inch master from which the album was made, dated January 3rd, 1975 – i.e. just four days after the final Minneapolis session – contains instructions about the speed, but clearly these were not adhered to, and no one, least of all Dylan, bothered to check to make sure his artistic decisions were respected.

One can enter into the whole debate about listening to the album Dylan intended, as opposed to the one he recorded, but the official releases (1981 halfspeed excepted) – which include the 2012 Mobile Fidelity vinyl – do neither job. One can only hope that when (or if) the New York test pressing is finally officially released, it will appear at its correct, i.e. natural, speed, as the Minneapolis tracks addended to the 6-CD version of *More Blood, More Tracks* now do.

What one does with the released album is more of a vexed question, as either three-tenths or seven-tenths of it, depending on your point of view, is still patently wrong. Given that the sped-up *Kind Of Blue* has been all but expunged from musical history, perhaps now is the time for the same to happen to the 'incorrect' *Blood On The Tracks* that has been sitting in record racks for the past 44 years.

Not So Much Born Again As Back Again

I can change, I swear; from a full-blown tome to monograph man this time around. Having foresworn completing the *Bootleg Series* trilogy, I have proven congenitally incapable of resisting writing *something* about *Blood On The Tracks*, specifically the New York *Blood On The Tracks*, once my appetite had been whetted by some of the recordings that had fallen by the wayside – all of which are about to become available on the deluxe edition of *More Blood, More Tracks*.

Inevitably, what began as a possible pitch for my first *Bootleg Series* sleeve-notes quickly became too large and too forensic for such a purpose (even if I could have persuaded the powers that be to let it be me). A trip to the Tulsa Dylan archives in March made my trajectory yet more diffuse until I began to think what a good idea it might be to revive the Wanted Man Study Series, a short-lived adjunct to *The Telegraph* we had inflicted on subscribers in the 1980s; which – if my memory serves me well – ran to half a dozen worthy monographs.

So here it is, the first volume in a sophomoric Wanted Man Study Series. Hopefully, there'll be more, from equally distinct voices in the near-virgin territory that is Dylan Studies. This one purports to tell the story of the 'New York' *Blood On The Tracks* – what happened, *et pourquoi*, filtered through the searing lens of hindsight with the full session tapes as my witness.

So, fulsome thanks to all of those who raided their memory banks for the cause: Glenn Berger, Rich Blakin, Tony Brown, Rob Fraboni, Barry Kornfeld, Kevin Odegard, Paul Rappaport, Pete Rowan, Larry Sloman and Steve Wilson. Especially fulsome thanks go to Ellen Bernstein, who for a third time endured my impertinent queries, and to whom this slim volume is respectfully dedicated.

I also salute those who oiled the wheels of investigation, directly or indirectly: Joel Bernstein, Mitch Blank, Susan Blond, Paul Burch, Zac Dadic, Peter Doggett, Parker Fishel, Robert Hilburn, Glenn

Korman, Ben Schafer, Peter Stone Brown and Thomas Tierney; while Mike DeCapite gave it the once over with a blue pen.

And, as ever, thanks to Jeff Rosen for green lights and insights; as well as to Mark Davidson and Michael Chaiken at the Dylan archive in Tulsa, Oklahoma, for assorted displays of generosity, spiritual and practical.

Clinton Heylin, June 2018.

WITH EACH NEW ALBUM, IT WAS A DIFFERENT DYLAN. AND THE QUESTION WAS ALWAYS POSED: WHICH IS THE REAL ONE? BUT OF COURSE THEY ALL WERE REAL. THEY WERE FILLED WITH THE TRUTH. BUT WHO WAS THE MAN WHO MADE THEM?

WE STUDIED HIS ENIGMATIC PHOTOGRAPHS, BUT THERE WERE NO CLUES IN THAT BRITTLE STARE. IN HIS INTERVIEWS, HE PUT US ON. IN HIS FILM, HE PUT US DOWN. HE WAS KING OF BAD BOYS, AND HE WAS ALWAYS IN IMPERIAL SECLUSION.

EVERY SO OFTEN HE'D COME OUT OF THE SHADOWS IN SOME BOLD NEW INCARNATION: WOODY G. DYLAN, COWBOY BOB, WOODSTOCK BOB, THE LEGEND-KILLER, THE LEGEND. AND THEN HE'D DISAPPEAR AGAIN.

NOW, SUDDENLY, HERE'S THIS STARTLINGLY *EXPOSED* FIGURE STANDING IN THE SUNLIGHT. COULD THIS BE "THE REAL BOB DYLAN"? WE STILL CAN'T KNOW.

BUT WE DO KNOW THERE'S SOMETHING PROFOUNDLY DIFFERENT ABOUT THIS ALBUM.

WE DON'T KNOW WHAT CHANGE HAS COME ABOUT IN DYLAN'S LIFE. MAYBE EVEN HE DOESN'T. IN ANY CASE, HE ISN'T SAYING.

BUT THERE'S EVIDENCE. AND YOU CAN JUDGE FOR YOURSELF.

BOB
DYLAN
BLOOD
ON
THE
TRACKS

ON COLUMBIA RECORDS AND TAPES

Clinton Heylin is one of the leading rock historians in the world, with over two dozen books to his name. These include biographies of Bob Dylan (*Behind The Shades*), Van Morrison (*Can You Feel The Silence?*), Bruce Springsteen (*E Street Shuffle*) and Sandy Denny (*No More Sad Refrains*), as well as his acclaimed pre-punk history, *From The Velvets To The Voidoids*, and the one and only history of rock bootlegs, *Bootleg*. His highly acclaimed titles *It's One For The Money* and *Anarchy In The Year Zero* were nominated for the Penderyn Book Award. Two recent titles, *JUDAS!* and *Trouble In Mind*, are in-depth accounts of the two electrifying periods in Bob Dylan's career when he was roundly booed. He lives in Somerset.

For more on this book, please visit:
www.route-online.com